The 4S Project:

Floor Three

By

Marshall Armstrong

Copyright © 2024 by Marshall D. Armstrong

The 4S Project

All rights reserved. No part of this publication may be reproduced, distributed, or transmitted in any form or by any means, including photocopying, recording, or other electronic or mechanical methods, without the prior written permission of the publisher, except in the case of brief quotations embodied in critical reviews and certain other noncommercial uses permitted by copyright law.

Although the author and publisher have made every effort to ensure that the information in this book was correct at press time, the author and publisher do not assume and hereby disclaim any liability to any party for any loss, damage, or disruption caused by errors or omissions, whether such errors or omissions result from negligence, accident, or any other cause.

This is a work of fiction. Names, businesses, characters, places, and incidents are the product of the author's imagination or used in a fictitious manner. Any resemblance to actual persons, living or dead, events, or locales is purely coincidental.

Adherence to all applicable laws and regulations, including international, federal, state and local governing professional licensing, business practices, advertising, and all other aspects of doing business in the US, Canada or any other jurisdiction is the sole responsibility of the reader and consumer.

Neither the author nor the publisher assumes any responsibility or liability whatsoever on behalf of the consumer or reader of this material. Any perceived slight of any individual or organization is purely unintentional.

Neither the author nor the publisher can be held responsible for the use of the information provided within this book.

Acknowledgments

I would like to thank my reviewers and all the people in my life that provided encouragement and inspiration. There are many friends and family members that made this possible by providing their unwavering support, inspiration, wisdom, and advice.

To you the reader: Thank you so much for choosing this book. I truly hope you have enjoyed the first two floors of the series.

Table of Contents

Main Characters 6

ACT 1 6

  SCENE 1: THE NEW GUYS 6

ACT 1 19

  SCENE 2: ZARLOW'S JOB 19

ACT 1 34

  SCENE 3: THE CONFRONTATION 34

ACT 2 51

  SCENE 1: GRANT MATCHES 51

ACT 2 63

  SCENE 2: MICHIYLA 63

ACT 2 80

  SCENE 3: CROSSROADS 80

ACT 3 99

  SCENE 1: ZARLOW MEETS HQ 99

ACT 3 114

  SCENE 2: XAXBEY'S SACRIFICE 114

ACT 3 129

  SCENE 3: ZARLOW'S CHOICE 129

Main Characters

Zarlow – 22-year-old, brown hair and brown eyes

Clariese – 24-year-old, blonde hair and green eyes

Everliegh – 26-year-old, red hair and blue eyes

Grant – 28-year-old, brown hair and hazel eyes

Yendizee – 22-year-old – black hair and brown eyes

Xaxbey – 23-year-old, brown hair and blue eyes

Ivirist – 24-year-old, blonde hair and hazel eyes

Julie-Ann – 26-year-old, sandy blonde hair and brown eyes

Michiyla – 21-year-old, dark brown hair and blue eyes

Braxton – 23-year-old, blonde hair and green eyes

Anthony – 27-year-old, dusty blonde hair and green eyes

Blake – 22-year-old – black hair and brown eyes

Stewart-Lee – 22-year-old – blonde hair and blue eyes

Koristine – 35-year-old – brown hair and brown eyes

Cook – Head of kitchen staff, tall, muscular,

Doc – Head of medical staff medium build

Other participants – many other participants of the program come in and out of each scene.

ACT 1

SCENE 1: THE NEW GUYS

(Enter Clariese, Julie-Ann, Xaxbey, Everliegh, Ivirist, Blake, and Zarlow)

(Clariese and Zarlow are sitting beside each other in the loveseat holding hands. Julie-Ann is relaxing in a chair, Xaxbey is sitting next to her in another armchair. Everliegh, Ivirist, and Blake are sitting on a couch. Julie-Ann looks around and then leans forward.)

JULIE-ANN: Where is Payshell? I don't see him anywhere. He is usually out here before us.

IVIRIST: Yes, you know what? I haven't seen him since we got to this floor.

JULIE-ANN: You don't think…

(Julie-Ann stops and looks at the others.)

BLAKE: Well, he wasn't really clicking with anyone. It's possible he didn't make it.

(Julie-Ann holds off the smile she so desperately wants to portray. She sits back and shakes her head in false sadness.)

JULIE-ANN: Man, that's too bad. I hope he is OK.

(Julie-Ann sees two guys coming toward the group. She points at them. Blake is the first to look over at them.)

(Enter Braxton and Anthony)

BLAKE: Hi, guys. What's up? I haven't seen you around here before.

BRAXTON: We were hanging out in the first sitting area on the first couple of floors. But we noticed a couple of our friends weren't around anymore since we got to Floor Three. So, we decided to walk around a bit and see what's all here in the building.

BLAKE: You can stay here and hang out with us.

(Blake looks around but doesn't see any chairs open.)

BRAXTON: That's cool of you. But I think you have all of the chairs occupied. Besides, we wanted to go over to the next room and check it out too.

(They start to head off, but Blake stops them.)

BLAKE: Hold on. I'll go grab some chairs from the next sitting area for you.

(Blake and Braxton head over and grab some chairs. When they come around the corner, Ivirist sees Blake struggling to carry a chair. Braxton, on the other hand, has the chair in one arm. Braxton's muscles are clearly seen, Ivirist stares at him and grins. Clariese looks at Braxton too. Julie-Ann notices the girls watching him intently. Julie-Ann

sits up and smiles. Julie-Ann crosses her legs, puts her elbow on her knee, and imagines how things just got a lot easier for her.)

JULIE-ANN: So. What happened over there that brought you guys to this sitting area?

BRAXTON: Well, on floors one and two, I thought I was hitting it off pretty good with lady. But when I got up here, I didn't see her. I've been walking around trying to see if she made it to this floor. Anthony and I thought we would wander over here and see if we could find her.

(Anthony nods in agreement.)

JULIE-ANN: There were girls from your group that didn't make it up here?

BRAXTON: It appears so. We can't find them.

IVIRIST: That makes sense. Payshell isn't here. Maybe he got bounced back too.

JULIE-ANN: I wonder how we find out who didn't make it.

IVIRIST: We should go look over there.

(Ivirist points to the other sitting areas.)

Maybe Payshell found a new group to be with.

JULIE-ANN: You stay here, I'll go look so it doesn't look too obvious.

IVIRIST: You sure?

(Ivirist looks at Braxton out of the corner of her eye. Julie-Ann smiles at her.)

JULIE-ANN: Yes. You stay here and chat. I'll be back in a few.

IVIRIST: OK. Let us know what you find out.

(Julie-Ann gets up and heads around over to the next sitting area. Once she is behind the wall separating the sitting areas, she touches her ear. She takes a quick look around. She sees a couple of people chatting in the chairs closest to the fireplace, but she figures it is safe to talk to HRS where she is at.)

JULIE-ANN: Good morning, HRS.

(Julie-Ann hears the normal static in her ear.)

KORISTINE: Good morning, Julie-Ann. Welcome to Floor Three. How's it going?

JULIE-ANN: I think it's starting off pretty good. Looks like I should be getting another bonus. Payshell didn't make it up here.

(Julie-Ann picks a piece of fuzz off of her shirt. She feels pride for the work she has done so far with this group.)

KORISTINE: I think you're right.

JULIE-ANN: And now two guys have come over and started talking with Ivirist, Everliegh, and Clariese. I'm gonna have a little bit of fun with this one.

KORISTINE: We saw Ivirist's heat signature go up a little.

JULIE-ANN: But not Clariese?

(Koristine points to a tech, covers the mic on her headset, and yells over at him.)

KORISTINE: Pull up Clariese.

(The tech puts Clariese's heat signature up on a tile. After a quick glance at the tile, Koristine uncovers the mic and talks to Julie-Ann.)

Julie-Ann, it looks like Clariese's heat signature was normal.

JULIE-ANN: Huh, OK. I saw her glance at one of the guys. I thought maybe she was getting a little excited too.

KORISTINE: It doesn't appear that way from here but keep your eyes open.

JULIE-ANN: OK. You know I'll work my magic.

(Julie-Ann touches her ear. She walks over to the first sitting area and looks around. While Julie-Ann is away,

Ivirist, Everliegh, Clariese, Blake, and Zarlow are talking with the new guys.)

EVERLIEGH: Where's Grant? And Where is Yendizee?

ANTHONY: Who are they?

EVERLIEGH: They used to hang out with us here. Do you think they didn't make it?

IVIRIST: Hardly. They are probably around the corner laughing at us.

BRAXTON: Were they a couple?

(Braxton flexes his muscles out of a subconscious reflex. Ivirist tilts her head and smiles. Zarlow looks at her. Then he looks over at Clariese. He notices she is staring at him too.)

IVIRIST: Ha! I doubt it.

EVERLIEGH: Wait a second, though. That makes sense. Weren't they getting a little closer right before we came up here?

(Ivirist sits back again trying to recall how they were acting. She can't really remember even though it was just a couple of days ago.)

IVIRIST: I guess it does.

(Clariese notices Julie-Ann leaning on the wall watching them.)

CLARIESE: Hi Julie-Ann. Did you see Payshell?

(Frustrated Clariese saw her, Julie-Ann walks over to the group.)

JULIE-ANN: Nope. Didn't see him at all. He must be gone.

CLARIESE: What about Grant or Yendizee?

JULIE-ANN: Nope. I didn't see them either. Are they not here?

IVIRIST: We haven't seen them.

JULIE-ANN: Should I go check on Yendizee again? I know where her room is.

BRAXTON: Ya. I'll go with you.

(He breaks out laughing knowing he can't go down the female hallway even though he would love to. Ivirist watches every breath he takes seeing his toned abs. She stares at him until she hears Julie-Ann talking and feels her hand on her shoulder.)

JULIE-ANN: Ivirist! Hey! Wake up!

IVIRIST: What? Ok. I'm Ok.

(The group chuckles at her.)

JULIE-ANN: I'll be back in a bit. I'm gonna go check on Yendizee.

(Julie-Ann stops right before she gets to the hallway leading to the rooms. She looks back at the group. She sees Ivirist and Clariese still staring at Braxton. She stores that information away for a later time. She heads a few steps down the hallway and touches her ear.)

HRS. Guess what?

KORISTINE: Hi, Julie-Ann. You are on comms an awful lot today.

JULIE-ANN: So much has happened that I was not informed about. We've been on Floor Three for a couple of days and you didn't tell me Payshell got bounced. That irritates me.

KORISTINE: There is a reason…

(Julie-Ann keeps talking.)

JULIE-ANN: And now, I find out Grant and Yendizee are nowhere to be found. Are they gone too? Why are you not telling me these things? I don't like surprises you know!

(Julie-Ann takes a breath.)

KORISTINE: Are you finished?

JULIE-ANN: Maybe. It depends on what you tell me.

KORISTINE: I can tell you Grant and Yendizee are on Floor Three. They are matching nicely.

(Julie-Ann stomps her foot,)

JULIE-ANN: Dang it! I thought I had them gone!

KORISTINE: Sorry. They are there somewhere.

JULIE-ANN: Fine. I need to go and stir up some trouble. See you later.

KORISTINE: Go get…

(Julie-Ann touches her ear cutting off Koristine, and heads back out. She stops just before the group can see her. She watches as Ivirist is still dreamily looking at Braxton. Clariese is no longer with the group. Zarlow is sitting twirling his index finger around his thumb. Julie-Ann walks over and sits down next to Zarlow. She whispers to him.)

JULIE-ANN: Where is Clariese?

ZARLOW: I think she went to get a drink.

JULIE-ANN: Did you see the way she was looking at the new guys?

ZARLOW: No.

JULIE-ANN: Seriously? I thought I saw her eyeing him.

ZARLOW: I doubt it.

(Zarlow sits back and looks at the wall. Julie-Ann musters the most caring tone of voice she can.

JULIE-ANN: Hey, I'm just looking out for you.

(Zarlow laughs knowing that she is the Destroyer.)

ZARLOW: Thanks. I appreciate it.

(Julie-Ann looks around for a second. She leans closer to Zarlow.)

JULIE-ANN: Look over there.

(Julie-Ann points to the drink machine off to the right of the long table with the snacks on it.)

ZARLOW: What?

JULIE-ANN: Do you see what I see? Clariese looks like she is smiling at Anthony right now. Look at them.

(Zarlow looks over at the drink machine. His mouth drops when he sees Clariese standing in front of Anthony grinning. Zarlow winces when Anthony runs his hand down Clariese's upper arm and touches her elbow. Zarlow gets up. Julie-Ann grabs his arm. She notices Clariese glance over, so Julie-Ann gently grabs Zarlow. Julie-Ann slowly runs her fingers down Zarlow's forearm and grabs his hand.)

You aren't gonna go fight him, are you? Don't do anything silly, Zarlow. You will get dismissed from the program.

ZARLOW: Nah. I'm gonna go be by myself for a while. See you later.

JULIE-ANN: Zarlow…

(He holds his hand up and walks off.)

IVIRIST: Is he OK?

JULIE-ANN: I think so. He probably needs a few minutes alone.

(Zarlow gets to his room and falls on his bed face first. Face down he starts talking.)

ZARLOW: I knew it was too good to be true. What a fool I was.

(Zarlow folds his pillow in half, lays on his back, puts his head on his pillow, and stares at the ceiling. Clariese and Anthony have rejoined the group in the sitting area.)

JULIE-ANN: Hey, welcome back.

(Ivirist has a thought pop into her head.)

IVIRIST: Hey, I just remembered. Didn't they say we could like, hold hands, and things like that on this floor?

JULIE-ANN: You're right. I think they did. That's a good point. Someone please start holding hands around here!

(The group laughs.)

CLARIESE: Ya, well, Julie-Ann. Why aren't you sitting next to Xaxbey?

(Julie-Ann mumbles a few inaudible words.)

XAXBEY: Yes, come over here and sit next to me. I will hold your hand.

(Xaxbey scoots over and slaps the cushion next to him. Julie-Ann glares at Clariese. Clariese ignores her. Clariese looks around for a second, puzzled that Zarlow isn't there anymore.)

CLARIESE: Where is Zarlow?

(Julie-Ann goes over and sits next to Xaxbey. Julie-Ann looks at Clariese.)

JULIE-ANN: Oh. He needed some time alone. I think he went back to his room.

ANTHONY: Do you want me to go get him?

CLARIESE: No. He will be back here in a little while. Thanks though.

(Clariese scoots back against the chair. She swings her feet hitting the chair leg every now and then.)

BRAXTON: So. Do you ever do more than just sit and talk?

IVIRIST: We haven't been allowed to do much more for the last couple of months.

BRAXTON: This is boring. I thought maybe things were different in this sitting area.

(Ivirist glares at Braxton.)

IVIRIST: You're shallow!

(The group laughs at Braxton. He rolls his eyes unamused.)

BRAXTON: Funny.

(Braxton looks around at the folks he just met.)

Let's do something fun. Does anyone want to do some pushups?

(Braxton gets on the ground and starts counting as he is doing pushups. Ivirist rolls her eyes. Clariese gets up and heads toward the hallway.)

JULIE-ANN: Clariese, you want me to go with you?

CLARIESE: No thanks. You all have fun. I'll be back later.

(Anthony watches as she leaves. He looks at Xaxbey.)

ANTHONY: Is she OK?

XAXBEY: Ya. She will be fine.

(The group continues chatting and cutting up, mostly poking fun at Braxton.)

END SCENE ONE

ACT 1

SCENE 2: ZARLOW'S JOB

(A few days have passed with nothing exciting happening. After waking up from a short nap on his bed, Zarlow grabs his device and starts looking around. Zarlow just gets into the mainframe, and the ballon chat emoji appears. Zarlow grumbles and pounds his fist into his bed.)

ZARLOW: Now what do you want?

(Zarlow clicks on the emoji. He hears Koristine's voice coming through the device.)

KORISTINE: Hi, Zarlow.

ZARLOW: Hello.

KORISTINE: I see you're back snooping around again.

ZARLOW: I thought I had permission to look around now.

KORISTINE: Not just yet. You haven't signed the NDA that is required for us to work together.

(Zarlow sees a document come through onto his device.)

ZARLOW: I see it now.

KORISTINE: Did you tell Clariese everything?

ZARLOW: No.

(Zarlow puts his palm on his forehead and rubs it.)

KORISTINE: Why not?

ZARLOW: She didn't meet me in the corner.

KORISTINE: Did you tell her it was important?

ZARLOW: No. I wasn't sure I wanted her to know.

KORISTINE: She doesn't have to know.

(Zarlow rubs his temples still visualizing the moment when he saw Anthony touch Clariese's arm.)

ZARLOW: It might not matter.

KORISTINE: Why? What are you talking about?

ZARLOW: I think Clariese likes someone else now.

(Zarlow waits for a response. The silence makes him uncomfortable, so Zarlow keeps talking.)

I saw her talking with another guy.

KORISTINE: Who?

ZARLOW: Some guy named Anthony. He rubbed her arm when he was talking to her. She smiled a lot. I could tell she liked it.

KORISTINE: Zarlow, hold on a second.

ZARLOW: OK.

(Zarlow puts his device down and closes his eyes. He ponders what campus he would go to next if he had to start over. Koristine looks down at the tech in front of her and points at her. Koristine pushes the mic on her headset away from her mouth so she can talk to the tech.)

KORISTINE: Tech, pull up Clariese on the tile. I want it on the large center tile please.

TECH: Uh, boss. We can't. She's in her room.

KORISTINE: Then pull up the visual of her when she was at the drinking station in sitting area three.

TECH: What timeframe?

(Koristine pulls her mic over so she can talk to Zarlow.)

KORISTINE: Hey, Zarlow. When was Clariese at the drinking station with Anthony?

(Zarlow is still pondering his future and doesn't hear Koristine. Koristine yells into the mic.)

                Zarlow!

(Zarlow is startled.)

ZARLOW: What?

KORISTINE: Listen to me! I'm trying to help you! When was Clariese with Anthony at the drinking station?

ZARLOW: Why? what does it matter? She found someone better than me. Let her be.

(Koristine slams her foot down on the platform. Three techs jump in their seats.)

KORISTINE: Because I asked you, that's why!

(Zarlow thinks back for a second.)

ZARLOW: About two days or so ago. Just about this time of day.

(Koristine looks at the tech and covers her mic.)

KORISTINE: Give me the timeframe for two days ago.

(The tech pulls up the image of Clariese and Anthony Koristine takes her hand off of the mic.)

OK, Zarlow. I see it here.

ZARLOW: Wait. You can see it? You have replay ability?

KORISTINE: Yes. Now stop interrupting me.

ZARLOW: OK. Sorry.

KORISTINE: I see Anthony with his hand on her shoulder.

ZARLOW: Yep, that's it. Maybe I should go find another campus. I was thinking…

(Koristine yells into the mic again.)

KORISTINE: Zarlow!

(She pauses. After a few seconds Koristine starts talking again in a more calming tone of voice.)

Calm down. Take a breath and let me finish.

(Zarlow waits as Koristine gives another pause. Koristine watches two minutes of the replay observing Clariese's interaction with Anthony.)

Just as I suspected.

ZARLOW: What? You can tell she likes him, can't you? Why did I even think I had a chance with her?

(Zarlow covers his face with his hands. He feels water well up in his eyes. Koristine speaks with a reassuring voice.)

KORISTINE: Listen to me carefully. I need you to relax. I want to tell you something, but you have to believe me. Can you do that?

ZARLOW: I don't know. Maybe.

KORISTINE: Zarlow, listen to me. Have I ever lied to you?

ZARLOW: No. Not yet.

KORISTINE: Listen to the words I'm about to say.

ZARLOW: OK.

(Zarlow takes his hands off of his face.)

KORISTINE: There is nothing romantic going on between Clariese and Anthony.

ZARLOW: How do you know?

KORISTINE: Once you sign that NDA and get your login you can find out all the details. I can tell you that the nanobots can read heat signatures and interpret them. I can tell by the signals relayed back to us by the nanobots that she is not romantically involved with Anthony. Are you ready to keep going?

ZARLOW: Maybe.

(Zarlow buries his head in his hands again. Koristine starts talking, but this time Koristine's voice turns more serious.)

KORISTINE: Zarlow, do you want to work with us, or not?

ZARLOW: Yes. I do.

KORISTINE: Are you gonna talk to Clariese?

ZARLOW: I doubt it.

KORISTINE: Just think about what I told you.

(Zarlow continues to rub his head.)

ZARLOW: When can I start this new job?

KORISTINE: Not until you get things worked out with Clariese.

(Zarlow looks up at the wall.)

ZARLOW: Why?

KORISTINE: You have to match to get to the next floor. I can't have you gain access to all of our stuff if you aren't continuing in the program and making an effort to complete the process.

ZARLOW: What about Julie-Ann? She seems to be trying to drive a wedge between Clariese and I. She's the one that noticed Clariese smiling at Anthony.

KORISTINE: Let me take care of that. I'll make sure she doesn't bother you anymore.

ZARLOW: But that's her job, right?

KORISTINE: It won't be. Trust me, I'll handle that from my end.

(Koristine looks at the tech monitoring Zarlow. The tech shakes her head. Koristine adjusts the mic on her headset.)

        Are you gonna sign the NDA?

(Zarlow pulls the NDA back up on his device.)

ZARLOW: Yes.

(Zarlow looks for a place to sign.)

        I don't see anywhere, or anyway, to sign.

KORISTINE: Turn the device over.

(Zarlow turns his device over. He watches as a place for his palm appears.)

ZARLOW: Whoa! How did you do that?

KORISTINE: Nanobots. Remember, Zarlow?

ZARLOW: Ya. I guess that makes sense.

KORISTINE: Place your palm on the device.

STEWART-LEE: Watch out! It's gonna hurt!

(Zarlow pulls his hand away from the device.)

ZARLOW: Who was that?

(Koristine motions for Stewart-Lee to keep his mouth shut.)

KORISTINE: That was just a coworker. You're fine, Zarlow. Go ahead and place your palm on the device.

(Zarlow holds his palm just above the hand-shaped indent on the device.)

ZARLOW: Will it hurt?

KORISTINE: Yes. But, only for a second.

(Zarlow slams his hand down on the device. He feels multiple stinging pinpricks all over the palm of his hand.)

ZARLOW: Ouch!

STEWART-LEE: Told you so!

(Koristine looks over at Stewart-Lee. He drops his head and walks down the platform steps. Stewart-Lee stops next to a tech working below and in front of the platform. He looks up at Koristine.)

> Sorry.

ZARLOW: Now what?

(Zarlow hears Koristine's voice change to more stern.)

KORISTINE: Now, and I mean right now, you are gonna go talk to Clariese and get things worked out.

ZARLOW: If that's even possible.

(Koristine ignores his comment.)

KORISTINE: Once you tell me you have talked to her, I'll have a tech open up your mainframe permissions.

(Zarlow giggles.)

What's so funny?

ZARLOW: I don't need your access codes. I've already been in your mainframe.

KORISTINE: Yes. But this way, you won't have to try and hack in. You can just log right into the programs you want.

ZARLOW: Any program?

KORISTINE: Yes.

(Zarlow rubs his chin.)

ZARLOW: Where can I talk to Clariese? What if she doesn't like me anymore? Then am I out of job?

KORISTINE: We will make sure you have a match. But I'm pretty sure Clariese is a safe bet.

ZARLOW: OK, I'll give it a shot. Where can I talk to her face-to-face without being conspicuous?

KORISTINE: Try the same corner again. I'll even turn off the nanobots again.

ZARLOW: Thank you.

KORISTINE: But Zarlow.

ZARLOW: Yes?

KORISTINE: This time talk to her. Or you're out of the program for good.

ZARLOW: Got it.

(Koristine covers the mic on her headset and looks at a tech below her and off to her right.)

KORISTINE: Tech, get Clariese to come out and meet Zarlow in the fourth sitting area. Turn off the nanobots in that area for an hour.

TECH: On it.

(Koristine takes her hand off the mic to talk to Zarlow again.)

KORISTINE: Zarlow.

ZARLOW: Yes.

KORISTINE: Be careful how much you tell Clariese. She seems tough, but it might be wise to be a bit careful.

ZARLOW: Thanks. When should I talk to her?

KORISTINE: The nanobots are off in that same corner again. I won't turn them on until I hear back from you.

ZARLOW: You and I can only communicate here, right?

KORISTINE: Yes.

ZARLOW: So, when I'm with the others, I just act normally?

KORISTINE: You got it. I hope you're a good actor.

(Koristine smiles.)

ZARLOW: I'll do my best.

(One of the techs holds a thumbs up.)

KORISTINE: Clariese is on her way out to one of the sitting areas. Go now and talk to her, Zarlow.

ZARLOW: OK. I'm off. Wish me luck.

(Zarlow puts his device back in its place. He shakes his head, does a little self-talk as he walks in circles, and then opens the door. Koristine snaps at the tech sitting right below the platform to get her attention.)

KORISTINE: Tech! Get me Julie-Ann.

TECH: One second.

(Koristine waits for a few moments. Then she sees the tech point at her.)

KORISTINE: Julie-Ann.

JULIE-ANN: Yes. Now what?

KORISTINE: I need you to lay off Clariese and Zarlow. We are going to let them match and go to the next floor together.

JULIE-ANN: What? You had me leave the group to tell me this? I was getting a good plan in place to have a few of those folks kicked out of the program!

KORISTINE: Well, get back in there and get them removed! Just leave Zarlow and Clariese alone.

JULIE-ANN: Why?

KORISTINE: Because I said so. Leave it at that.

JULIE-ANN: You are taking a lot of credits away from me. I was working on them just now!

KORISTINE: I know. But I want you to stop.

JULIE-ANN: And lose credits? What's going on?

KORISTINE: Never mind that. I'll have the credits deposited into your account right now.

(Koristine points up to a small office above the platform Koristine stands on. The office is surrounded by glass and is off to the left of the main entrance of the EYECom building. Stewart-Lee follows Koristine's gaze and sees the glass office. He scratches his head.)

STEWART-LEE: I never saw that before?

(Dismayed, Koristine looks at Stewart-Lee.)

KORISTINE: Shhhhh.

(Koristine sees the office worker wave. Koristine turns her attention back to Julie-Ann.)

OK, Julie-Ann. The money is deposited. Now go do your job!

JULIE-ANN: Fine. Anyone else I need to not touch? I would like to know before a spend energy on a plan and then get told to stop,

(Julie-Ann puts her hands on her hips and shakes her head.)

KORISTINE: Nope. They are all fair game.

(Relieved and happy, Julie-Ann smiles already having plans formulate in her mind.)

JULIE-ANN: Sweet.

(Julie-Ann heads back out to the group. She scratches her head wondering why Zarlow is off limits.)

STEWART-LEE: So, the person up there is listening to us at all times?

KORISTINE: Yep. They hear everything that is going on here.

(Stewart-Lee stares up at the glass box. He wonders what it would be like working up there, hearing everything that goes on across the whole compound.)

END SCENE TWO

ACT 1

SCENE 3: THE CONFRONTATION

(Zarlow is sitting in the far corner waiting for Clariese. After a few moments pondering how he will bring up the subjects he needs to discuss, Zarlow puts his head down. He pulls his knees up almost to his chest and rests his elbows on his knees. Zarlow puts his head in his hands pondering what he will do if Clariese does not want to be with him anymore. Zarlow plays out all the possible scenarios. He shakes his head and starts talking to himself.)

ZARLOW: Maybe I should just leave. Let her have a good life with someone better than me.

(Clariese sees Zarlow sitting in the corner just as the anonymous message on her device said he would be. She walks over to him, notices he doesn't realize she is there, and listens to him mumbling. She listens in as he murmurs under his breath.)

She would probably be better off with him. He's better looking. And he's probably smarter too. I'm a loser. Always have been…always will be.

(Clariese puts her hand on her hips. Feeling frustrated that Zarlow would think such things, she waits for him to look up. After what seems like eternity, Zarlow still has his hands over his head. So, she reaches down and touches his shoulder.)

CLARIESE: Zarlow.

(Zarlow flinches from being startled. He looks up and sees Clariese.)

        Sorry.

ZARLOW: Oh. Hi, Clariese.

CLARIESE: That's it? Oh, hi.

ZARLOW: Sorry.

(Zarlow gets up and steps toward her to hug her. She moves back a few steps.)

CLARIESE: What's going on here?

ZARLOW: I think we need to talk.

(Zarlow sits back down. He waits to see if she will sit next to him.)

CLARIESE: I have a bad feeling about this.

ZARLOW: I have a few things I need to tell you.

CLARIESE: OK.

(Zarlow pats the ground next to him. Clariese moves closer, but then stops. She shakes her head.)

ZARLOW: Please sit next to me.

CLARIESE: I heard you, Zarlow. I heard you talking to yourself just now.

ZARLOW: You were listening and didn't stop me?

CLARIESE: Yes.

(Zarlow rubs the back of his head with both of his hands.)

ZARLOW: Great. How much worse can this get?

CLARIESE: Zarlow, tell me what's going on.

ZARLOW: Do you…

(Zarlow stops. He's not sure whether to ask her if she likes Anthony first, or to tell her about his new agreement with 4S.)

CLARIESE: Yes. What?

ZARLOW: Please sit. I'm feeling nervous.

(Clariese rolls her eyes and sits down in a huff.)

CLARIESE: OK, I'm here.

(Zarlow looks over at her. He grabs her hand. She tries to pull it away, but he holds on to it tighter.)

ZARLOW: I need to ask you about earlier when you were standing with Anthony.

(A puzzled look comes over Clariese's face.)

CLARIESE: Who?

(Zarlow looks at her a little sterner.)

ZARLOW: The new guy.

(Zarlow lets go of her hand.)

You were standing with him by the drinking machine.

(Clariese rolls her eyes.)

CLARIESE: So.

ZARLOW: I saw him touch your shoulder.

CLARIESE: What? That's what this is about?

ZARLOW: And I saw him rub your elbow. Kinda like in a romantic way.

CLARIESE: So what?

ZARLOW: And you smiled at him.

(Zarlow looks away. Clariese gets up.)

CLARIESE: Seriously. Are you worried about that?

ZARLOW: Ya. I guess I am.

(Clariese puts her hands on her hips and looks down at Zarlow.)

CLARIESE: Seriously, after all we've been through already. Everything we have said to each other, and all the time we spent together. You think I'm falling for another guy?

(Zarlow raises his hand to start to speak but Clariese keeps going.)

You know what, Zarlow, I think maybe you are trying to get rid of me. Am I not good enough for you? Am I too short, or not pretty enough? Am I boring? If you don't want to be with me, just tell me. You promised me that much months ago. Ugh!

(Clariese walks in circles right in front of Zarlow.)

ZARLOW: Clariese….

(She stops directly in front of him and interrupts him.)

CLARIESE: I knew this would happen. You are trying to find a way out. Just like all the other guys in my life have. Why don't you just leave me alone, Zarlow. This stupid program doesn't work!

(Clariese stomps off and heads toward the hallway to her room. Zarlow gets up and runs to catch up with her. He grabs her arm gently.)

ZARLOW: Clariese. Please stop.

(She turns around and looks at him. She yanks her arm free and starts down the hallway. Zarlow catches up with her again and grabs her other arm a bit more tightly this time. She turns and yells at him.)

CLARIESE: Zarlow! Stop!

(Zarlow points to the wall. Clariese finally notices he is in the hallway to the ladies' rooms, and no one has come to get him. He looks into her eyes and speaks gently.)

ZARLOW: My Clar Star.

CLARIESE: How? Why? You shouldn't be here. This is impossible.

(Back at EYECom, a tech yells for Koristine.)

TECH: Hey! Uh, boss.

(Koristine turns to look at the tech. The tech puts the visual of Zarlow and Clariese in the hallway up on the center tile.)

KORISTINE: Yes?

(The tech points at the tile.)

TECH: You want me to call the guards?

(Koristine watches for a second. She makes sure they are both not headed for Clariese's room.)

KORISTINE: No. Let them be.

TECH: You sure?

KORISTINE: Yes. Take that off the tile.

(The tech pulls down the visual and puts up sitting area one on the tile. Clariese is still trying to figure out how Zarlow is able to be in the hallway with her.)

CLARIESE: What is going on?

(Zarlow moves closer to her.)

ZARLOW: I have so much I need to tell you, but I don't have a lot of time. Can we go back out there and sit in the corner again? Please.

(Clariese crosses her arms across her chest.)

CLARIESE: Tell me one thing. Truthfully.

ZARLOW: I promise.

CLARIESE: Only the truth.

ZARLOW: Yes. Just the truth.

CLARIESE: You owe me that much.

ZARLOW: Anything you want to know.

CLARIESE: Are you trying to get rid of me?

ZARLOW: No.

(Zarlow kisses Clariese. Stunned, she stands there. Zarlow turns around and walks back out to the corner. He sits down in the same spot and waits. Clariese comes out a few seconds later.)

CLARIESE: What was that?

ZARLOW: The truth.

(Clariese sits down next to him.)

CLARIESE: You have anything else you need to say.

(Clariese rubs her lips, half wanting him to kiss her again.)

ZARLOW: I have so many things I have to tell you, and I only have a limited time.

(Clariese covers her mouth. Then she whispers to him.)

CLARIESE: You're dying?

ZARLOW: What? ... No!

(Clariese slowly lets out the breath she was holding.)

We need to talk about you and Anthony.

CLARIESE: Not this again!

ZARLOW: I told you the truth. Now it's your turn.

(Clariese gets up again and stands over Zarlow.)

CLARIESE: The truth, Zarlow. You want the truth? The truth is he was talking about you and me.

(Zarlow closes his eyes.)

He told me how he thought you and I made a cute couple. He told me that he was so impressed how we could be so close in such a short amount of time. He wasn't hitting on me, Zarlow. He is happy for us. He told me how he hopes he finds the same kind of love he saw in you and me. He said he could tell right away we were meant to be together. You want the truth? That's the truth!

(Zarlow hangs his head. Then he remembers how she looked at Braxton.)

ZARLOW: What about Braxton? You looked at him and smiled. He has big muscles, maybe even the perfect body.

(Clariese starts walking toward the hallway again. She stops right before the doorway and turns around. She quickly walks back over to where Zarlow is sitting and stands over him.)

CLARIESE: Really, Zarlow? Really? You seriously do not trust me, do you? Braxton, of all people.

(Completely frustrated, Clariese lets out a yell.)

Aawwwwww!

ZARLOW: I…

CLARIESE: No, Zarlow. I will explain this one too, since you seemingly don't trust me.

ZARLOW: I'm....

(Clariese waves her hand in front of him and interrupts him again.)

CLARIESE: No, Zarlow. Hush.

(Zarlow looks at the ground between his legs. Half frustrated and half angry, Clariese raises her voice again.)

Look at me! You want the truth. You want to talk about this. Then you need to look at me!

(Zarlow sheepishly looks up at her.)

That Braxton guy is a self-absorbed, egotistical, jerk. I was not smiling at him!

ZARLOW: You weren't?

CLARIESE: You interrupt me one more time and I'm leaving. Shut up and listen!

(Zarlow instinctively closes his mouth.)

I wasn't smiling at Braxton. You know what I was smiling about?

(Zarlow remains silent and shakes his head.)

I was smiling because I was thinking how lucky I was to have a guy like you. Not some self-loving, shallow....

(Clariese lets out a huff as she gets worked up.)

...nimrod! That's what he is! He's a nimrod! No, Zarlow. I was not thinking that he is hot, or whatever you thought I was dreaming about. I was thinking about how much I love you!

(Tears well up in Clariese's eyes.)

ZARLOW: Really?

(Clariese nods and wipes the tears from her eyes with her blouse. Zarlow gets up and stands in front of her.)

I'm sorry. I was scared.

CLARIESE: Never question me again.

(Clariese hugs him.)

Promise me.

(Zarlow hugs her tighter than he ever has.)

ZARLOW: I promise.

(After hugging for a while, Clariese pushes back just a little.)

CLARIESE: Wait a minute! Tell me how you got halfway down the ladies' hallway and didn't get in trouble. And how are we able to hug for so long and not get caught? And how did you know you could kiss me?

ZARLOW: That is the other part I need to talk to you about.

CLARIESE: There's more?

ZARLOW: Yes, and it concerns you.

(Clariese puts her hands on her hips again.)

CLARIESE: Zarlow, what did you do?

(Zarlow sits back down. Clariese looks down at him for a second. Zarlow pats the floor next to him and waits for her to sit. Eventually, she sits next to him. She grabs his hand and looks into his eyes waiting for an answer.)

ZARLOW: Remember when we talked, right here, in this corner?

CLARIESE: Yes.

ZARLOW: Well, come to find out, they caught me snooping in the mainframe.

CLARIESE: Oh, no! Zarlow, are you leaving the program? Not now. Ugh!

(Zarlow sees tears start to form in her eyes again. He squeezes her hand tightly. She looks away trying to contain her emotions.)

ZARLOW: No. In fact, the exact opposite.

(Confused, Clariese looks at Zarlow.)

CLARIESE: What?

ZARLOW: They offered me a job.

(Clariese leans away from Zarlow,)

CLARIESE: They what?

ZARLOW: I signed the NDA. I just have to tell you and then report back to them, and then I'm in. I will have access to everything. All their top-secret programs and coding.

CLARIESE: What? I don't understand.

(Zarlow takes a deep breath and squeezes Clariese's hand again.)

ZARLOW: They caught me getting further into the mainframe than anyone has ever gotten before. So, they offered me a job to create code so no one can ever do that again.

CLARIESE: Wow. Umm. I'm not sure what to say.

(Clariese leans into Zarlow.)

ZARLOW: I told you about Julie-Ann.

CLARIESE: Yes, and how she is a Destroyer like I was.

ZARLOW: Yep, she is the one that pointed out to me that Anthony was touching your arm.

CLARIESE: And you believed her? Zarlow! You know what she is! Now I'm frustrated again!

ZARLOW: I know. I get it.

(Clariese pulls her hand away from Zarlow and crosses her arms across her chest.)

CLARIESE: Do you?

(Zarlow looks straight ahead. Clariese looks away from him.)

ZARLOW: Clariese. I like you.

(She turns her head to look at him. Zarlow turns and looks her in the eye.)

No. I love you.

(Zarlow pauses. He puts his hand on Clariese's knee.)

I need you to listen to me.

(Clariese shakes her head as if trying to shake cobwebs out of her mind. Then she nods to Zarlow.)

CLARIESE: OK.

ZARLOW: I am going to work for the 4S Project. But that means I am gonna know everything. I won't be able to tell you things. Some things you ask about, I won't be able to give good answers. I need you to understand that. If you don't think it will work, please tell me now.

CLARIESE: You will get to know everything?

ZARLOW: I think so. Complete access to all their files and programs.

CLARIESE: What will you be doing?

ZARLOW: Writing programs to prevent hackers from gaining access. I think.

CLARIESE: And you know the coding they use?

ZARLOW: Mostly. They're using an EBTC-/+ Code which is a lot like the old C++ with a little Python mixed in.

CLARIESE: I have no idea what that means.

ZARLOW: Let me see.

(Zarlow scratches his head.)

I am going to take their current programs and add a little Bio-Nano code into their program to try and prevent anyone from getting the 4S confidential information.

CLARIESE: I see. I think. Well, not really. I'll just take your word for it.

ZARLOW: I just need to know that you will be OK with me not telling you everything that I work on.

CLARIESE: Fine. If you trust me and believe me when I say that I'm not flirting with any of the other guys.

(Clariese uncrosses her arms and puts her hand on Zarlow's.)

We have to trust each other if we want this relationship to go any further.

ZARLOW: I agree.

(Zarlow leans over and hugs Clariese. She wraps her arms around him. Zarlow kisses her neck. The sensation sends butterflies through Clariese's whole body.)

END ACT ONE

ACT 2

SCENE 1: GRANT MATCHES

(Enter Braxton, Anthony, Ivirist, Everliegh, Blake, Grant, Yendizee, Julie-Ann, and Xaxbey)

(Xaxbey and Julie-Ann are sitting together in the love seat. Ivirist sits next to Anthony in the armchair. Blake, Yendizee, Braxton, and Everliegh sit on a long couch. Grant sits in a chair he pulled over from another sitting area. He placed the chair at the end of the couch next to Everliegh.)

BLAKE: You answered the survey that way? Are you trying NOT to find a match?

YENDIZEE: What? I was just being honest. Wouldn't you rather match with someone being true to yourself than being together with someone who is fake?

(Xaxbey moves his hand right next to Julie-Ann's in the chair. He rubs her hand with his little finger. Without realizing it, Julie-Ann rubs his hand back. Xaxbey puts three fingers on her hand. She intertwines her little finger and ring finger with his. None of the others notice. Xaxbey smiles. Blake continues the conversation.)

BLAKE: Sure. But that is very blunt.

(Xaxbey has now grabbed Julie-Ann's hand. Julie-Ann hears static in her ear and then a voice.)

TECH: Julie-Ann, your heat signature is rising. You really like this guy!

(Julie-Ann realizes what happened and slowly pulls her hand away from Xaxbey. She turns her head and whispers,)

JULIE-ANN: Stop it.

(Xaxbey looks at her. He whispers back.)

XAXBEY: Sorry.

(Julie-Ann looks his way for a quick second and then whispers.)

JULIE-ANN: Not you.

(Xaxbey touches her hand again. Julie-Ann doesn't pull her hand away. Blake notices Julie-Ann and Xaxbey whispering to each other.)

BLAKE: Julie-Ann, are you two, OK?

JULIE-ANN: Huh?

(It takes Julie-Ann a second to realize what Blake is talking about.)

Oh. Ya. Everything is fine. I was just giving Xaxbey a hard time.

(Julie-Ann gives a fake laugh. Xaxbey smiles.)

GRANT: What? What happened?

BLAKE: Grant, sometimes you are so oblivious.

(The group laughs at Grant.)

GRANT: Ya. Ya. Laugh it up. Hardy har, har.

EVERLIEGH: Don't worry, Grant. I have no idea what's going on either.

(Grant smiles at Everliegh. She smiles back at him. Yendizee finds herself staring at Braxton. For some reason, she has not been able to keep her eyes off of Braxton since he showed up in this sitting area.)

YENDIZEE: So, Braxton. Did you answer the survey honestly?

BRAXTON: Of course. Well. I may have embellished in some areas.

(Braxton sits up a little and puts his shoulders back. He flexes his pectoral muscles out of habit. Yendizee watches in awe. Without knowing what she is doing, she smiles at him. Everliegh looks at Yendizee.)

EVERLIEGH: You trust him?

YENDIZEE: Yes. I do.

EVERLIEGH: You haven't trusted anyone yet. Then he shows up, and viola?

YENDIZEE: I can't explain it.

BRAXTON: You can trust me.

(Braxton smiles, leans back, and puts his hands behind his head. Everliegh rolls her eyes in disgust.)

EVERLIEGH: Yendizee, you can't be believing all this.

(Yendizee shrugs.)

YENDIZEE: I can't explain it. I trust him.

(Yendizee looks at the ground. Julie-Ann watches Yendizee noticing this is not how Yendizee usually acts.)

JULIE-ANN: Well. That would be an unexpected match.

(Everyone looks at Julie-Ann with perplexed looks.)

What? I'm just making an observation.

XAXBEY: Kinda cute. Aren't they?

(No one says anything. There is an uncomfortable silence in the room. Blake speaks up to break up the uncomfortable silence.)

BLAKE: I hope we all get a match. This is the last floor for goofing off. If we don't have a possible partner, we get bounced.

EVERLIEGH: Right? I hope that personality survey we just took at least gives us better insights.

BLAKE: How? We don't know how anyone else scored.

EVERLIEGH: Fair point. So then, how is that survey supposed to help us? Why did we even do it now? It seems like a waste of time to me.

XAXBEY: Maybe they use it on the next floor? To help us, you know, get confirmation of who we are supposed to be with.

IVIRIST: Then why not just tell us now? Why all of this waiting around? What if I match better with someone like...

(Ivirist looks around to hide her true feelings.)

...like, Anthony.

YENDIZEE: Ha! So! You like Anthony now! We found you out!

(Ivirist feels herself blush.)

ANTHONY: I'd be OK with that.

(Anthony looks over at Ivirist and smiles. Ivirist smiles back and looks at the ground.)

YENDIZEE: Oh, good grief! We are all acting like a bunch of fifth graders! If we like someone, we shouldn't be embarrassed about it. We are here to find a partner and start a family. We only have a few weeks until this crap becomes real. Don't we need a match to go to Floor Four?

(Yendizee points at Ivirist.)

Ivirist, we are at the point now, if you like Anthony just say so!

IVIRIST: I don't know, we just met.

BLAKE: Whatever. We all see how you look at each other. You never looked at me or Grant like that.

(The group all nods in unison. Yendizee points around the room and then holds her hand out toward Ivirist.)

YENDIZEE: We all can see it. Why can't you?

BLAKE: I just wished we knew what it took for sure to get to the next floor.

(An awkward silence comes over the group again. Clariese looks at Zarlow. He nods. Clariese chimes in having been on Floor Four previously.)

CLARIESE: It was a while ago, but when I was on Floor Three, the only way to get to the next floor was with a match.

IVIRIST: Who decides if we match or not?

(Clariese leans forward.)

CLARIESE: I'm not sure about that. Maybe we have a part in deciding that. And maybe the 4S folks help decide that too.

IVIRIST: So, how are we gonna know if we get to keep going? We just 'hope' that we make it, is that it?

ZARLOW: Ya, they haven't been super clear about that.

IVIRIST: What if we are faking it? How will they know?

(Clariese leans back in her chair.)

CLARIESE: From what I can tell, they know. Whoever 'they' are.

(Zarlow leans back and puts his arm around Clariese.)

ZARLOW: When I get to my room tonight, I'll read in the manual and see if I can find anything out.

GRANT: Well, be sure to let us know if you find anything.

ZARLOW: OK. If I see anything that might answer some of your questions, I'll let you know.

(Everliegh nods her head and chimes in.)

EVERLIEGH: Yes, anything that might help would be great. I definitely want to go to the next floor, but only with the right person.

GRANT: How do you know who the right person is? Doesn't that take years to really know?

IVIRIST: Unless you just know. Sometimes you can just tell.

EVELIEGH: Isn't it possible to grow into a relationship too?

(Everliegh looks at Grant. He smiles at her.)

IVIRIST: Sure, I think that's possible. But do we really have time for that now? I mean, we are kinda on the clock; so to speak.

EVERLIEGH: Yes, we kinda are, aren't we?

GRANT: Well then, I sure hope these 4S folks know what they are doing.

EVERLIEGH: Maybe we can help them out a little. You know, assist in making their decision?

(Everliegh looks at Grant. She puts her hand on the arm of the couch. Grant takes the hint and grabs her hand. Grant feels her soft skin against his. A desire for her that he has never felt before comes over him.)

YENDIZEE: See, that's what I'm talking about!

(Yendizee points at Everliegh and Grant.)

If you like someone, just show it!

(Grant squeezes Everliegh's hand. She squeezes his in return.)

IVIRIST: Everliegh, after more than a few months together, you know what Grant is like. If you like him, I say go for it.

GRANT: What is that supposed to mean?

(Everliegh squeezes his hand. She looks at him and winks.)

EVERLIEGH: Yes, I know what Grant is like. Sometimes he comes off shallow. He can seem a bit arrogant. But as I got to know him, I realized he really isn't those things. He is caring and considerate. I think he just puts on a persona to protect his tender and amazing heart.

(Everliegh blows Grant a kiss.)

IVIRIST: That's so sweet. I bet Grant wants to kiss you right now.

(Grant squirms in his seat feeling uneasy.)

GRANT: I probably would, if it was allowed.

EVERLIEGH: Awwww. Thanks. I'd kiss you right back.

(Everliegh puckers up her lips.)

Mwah!

(Everliegh watches as Grant turns bright red.)

YENDIZEE: See, that's cool right there. That's how I can tell it's authentic.

EVERLIEGH: I know my feelings are real. But I tell you, if you had told me on day one that I would fall for Gramps, I would have laughed you right out of the building.

(Julie-Ann struggles to form a new plan. She tries to hide her desire to get more of these folks to quit the program.)

JULIE-ANN: If you told us anyone would fall for Grant, we would all have called you a liar.

GRANT: Wow! Thanks everyone!

(They all laugh at Grant.)

Good thing I am self-confident.

EVERLIEGH: It is one of the many traits we love about you.

IVIRIST: Speak for yourself.

(Everliegh looks at Grant.)

EVERLIEGH: OK, I will. I love that trait of yours.

(Everliegh winks at him again.)

JULIE-ANN: Oh, c'mon Ivirist. I seriously thought you and Grant would end up being together.

(Ivirist looks over at Julie-Ann.)

IVIRIST: Really?

(Shocked, Grant chimes in, too.)

GRANT: Are you kidding?

JULIE-ANN: I'm serious!

EVERLIEGH: Honestly, I thought that the first few weeks as well.

(Everliegh smiles at Grant.)

IVIRIST: Wow, I guess I totally missed something back then.

EVERLIEGH: Too bad. He's mine now.

(Ivirist laughs.)

IVIRIST: He's all yours my friend.

EVERLIEGH: Well. Thanks for your permission.

(Grant throws his one free hand into the air.)

GRANT: Geeze, thanks for letting me have a choice too.

IVIRIST: Hey, you two have my blessing. I hope you prosper and have a huge family.

(The group laughs again.)

GRANT: Me too!

(Everliegh giggles.)

YENDIZEE: I'll toast to that! Oh wait. We don't have any drinks.

BRAXTON: I'll go get some. What does everyone want?

GRANT: Since I'm the Gramps here, I say bring us all back a soda.

(Everyone smiles as they all look at Grant. Yendizee gets up.)

YENDIZEE: I'll go with you.

(Yendizee and Braxton leave for the drink machine. Grant smiles at Everliegh. He rubs her hand with his. He stops right below her elbow. Everliegh reaches over with her other hand and puts it on his.)

XAXBEY: Now, let's make sure the rest of us get a match. I would love to go to Floor Four with all of you.

(Zarlow looks around the room.)

ZARLOW: Ya, that's a great idea.

(Zarlow looks at Clariese.)

If we can help in any way, just let us know. We like this group we have.

(Xaxbey looks at Julie-Ann. Julie-Ann smiles hesitantly. She would like that too. But that might be the end of her job with 4S. How can she balance feeling this way about Xaxbey, but also knowing she has a job to do?)

END SCENE ONE

ACT 2

SCENE 2: MICHIYLA

(Julie-Ann, Xaxbey, Grant, Ivirist, Blake, Anthony, Yendizee, Braxton, and Everliegh are hanging out in a sitting area. It's been a few days since they were talking about the survey results. Now they are discussing childhood memories. Blake looks up. His heart almost stops. He sees a beautiful woman heading their way. He straightens up on the couch and scoots over a bit.)

BLAKE: Hi. Um. I'm Blake.

(Blake hesitates and looks around. He pats the seat next to him.)

You can sit over here with me.

(The group all looks over at him almost in unison. Then they look in the direction of Blake's gaze. They see a new person standing near them. Julie-Ann speaks up next.)

JULIE-ANN: Hi. I'm Julie-Ann.

MICHIYLA: Hi. I'm Mi-Kiy-la. I saw you sitting over here and thought I'd come over. I hope that's OK.

JULIE-ANN: The more the merrier. Right, Blake.

(Blake glares at Julie-Ann for a second. Then he looks at Michiyla and he relaxes.)

BLAKE: Ya. You know what? I think you're right.

(Blake looks at Julie-Ann and points at her.)

But don't let that go to your head.

(The group chuckles a little.)

JULIE-ANN: Whatever, Blake. You dork.

(Blake laughs at her.)

BLAKE: Ha! Takes one to know one!

(Julie-Ann smiles.)

JULIE-ANN: Very funny. Way to pull an old childhood saying into the conversation. You're still a dork, though.

BLAKE: Michiyla, come sit down. Join this group of misfits.

(Everyone smiles knowing the truth of what Blake says.)

MICHIYLA: Thanks.

(Michiyla smiles at the group and sits down next to Blake. Blake can smell her. She smells so good. He feels his heart start racing.)

BLAKE: I haven't seen you around here before. I know I usually sit over here and don't venture around to the other sitting areas much, so that's probably the reason.

(Michiyla smiles at him.)

MICHIYLA: Ya. I was hanging out over in the second sitting area. But I didn't really get along with anyone over there. I felt like an odd person out a lot.

BLAKE: I know that feeling.

(Yendizee looks over at him. Perplexed, she stares at him for a second. Then she shrugs her shoulders and looks at Braxton. He winks at her.)

JULIE-ANN: So, you didn't really like anyone over there?

(Julie-Ann points at the area next door.)

MICHIYLA: I did, at first. But then something happened to the guy I thought I liked. When I got to this floor, he was gone. I couldn't find him anywhere.

ZARLOW: Who was it?

MICHIYLA: His name was Franklin.

(Zarlow looks at Clariese. She smiles and nods. Clariese sees in Zarlow's eyes the desire to go look through the mainframe for what happened to Franklin. Clariese taps Zarlow's hand twice. He grabs her hand and smiles at her.)

JULIE-ANN: That name sounds familiar.

(Julie-Ann scratches her chin trying to remember why she remembers that name. She hears tech chime in.)

TECH: That's one of the guys you tried to get dismissed. That was a while ago. I think back on Floor One. I'll look into it and let you know what happened to him.

(Julie-Ann hears the tech turn the mic off. Julie-Ann smiles, knowing she got another one removed. She sits back and grins even bigger now. Xaxbey interrupts her visual of Franklin getting removed on her account.)

XAXBEY: I'm so sorry, Michiyla. I'm sure you'll find someone before we move up to the next floor.

(Julie-Ann looks over at Xaxbey. He smiles at her. She smiles back. Michiyla looks at the ground in front of her.)

MICHIYLA: Thanks. But I'm not so sure. There just isn't a lot of time left for me I'm afraid.

BLAKE: Don't give up so easily. You're here for a reason. Your DNA matched with someone's. If your DNA match was gone, you wouldn't be here still, right?

MICHIYLA: I guess so.

(A little grin crosses Blake's face.)

BLAKE: What happened on the last floor? Why did the guy you thought you liked not make it up here? Do you know?

(Julie-Ann looks at Blake and holds her hand up in an effort to get him to slow down.)

JULIE-ANN: Dude, slow down with the questions.

(Julie-Ann looks at Michiyla.)

Are you gonna be, OK? If you ever need someone to talk to, I'm here.

(Michiyla looks at Julie-Ann and nods.)

MICHIYLA: Thank you. Really. I appreciate it.

(Michiyla looks at Blake. She smiles at him. Blake smiles back and leans forward toward her a little.)

BLAKE: I'm sorry I ask so many questions. It's just…

(Julie-Ann interrupts him.)

JULIE-ANN: It's just the way he is. He over questions everything.

BLAKE: She's not wrong. I do that a lot.

(Blake sits back in the chair and tries to let his emotions calm down for a moment.)

JULIE-ANN: Yes, you do. It might put some people off.

(Grant sits up a little and chimes in.)

GRANT: For real! That's probably why you don't have anyone right now. How did you make it to this floor anyway?

(Blake looks straight ahead and just shrugs his shoulders.)

BLAKE: You know. I'm not sure.

JULIE-ANN: You can always opt out. Quit, maybe.

BLAKE: Maybe.

JULIE-ANN: There's no judgement here, you know. We have all been there.

(Julie-Ann looks around the room. A few in the group nod their heads. Xaxbey, about to interject, hears the static in his ear. Then, a voice comes through his comms.)

HIS: Xaxbey, it looks like Blake and Michiyla might have something going. She is watching him constantly. More than that, he is the one she is looking at most of the time.

(Hearing this from HIS, Xaxbey jumps in.)

XAXBEY: Oh, c'mon, Blake. Hang in there. We've hung out a lot the last few months. You never gave up this easily before. Don't start that bad habit now.

HIS: Keep going. We are getting more information on Michiyla.

(Julie-Ann interjects trying to convince him to quit.)

JULIE-ANN: Still, sometimes we just need a fresh start. You know, kind of like a re-do. There is nothing wrong with it. You gave it a good shot here. You know…

(Xaxbey hears HIS again as Julie-Ann is talking.)

HIS: Keep them two talking with each other.

JULIE-ANN: …and so a fresh start somewhere else might be just what the doctor…

(Xaxbey lightly nudges Julie-Ann with his elbow and interrupts her.)

XAXBEY: Hey, Michiyla, we are glad you came over here and sat down. We are a pretty cool group.

(Michiyla looks at Blake unable to take her eyes off of him.)

So, back to Blake's question. Why did your friend not make it up here?

MICHIYLA: I have no idea.

(Frustrated, Julie-Ann glares a little at Xaxbey.)

JULIE-ANN: We don't need to bore her with all of these questions. She just got here, let's give her a break.

(Julie-Ann looks over at Michiyla.)

I would apologize for Blake, but that's just how he is I'm afraid.

(Michiyla looks at Julie-Ann and nods. Then she looks back at Blake.)

BLAKE: I'll try not to ask so many questions.

JULIE-ANN: No, you won't! That's just not your nature. You are just naturally inquisitive.

MICHIYLA: It's OK. I kinda like it.

(Julie-Ann and Blake both look at her simultaneously.)

BLAKE: What?

JULIE-ANN: Why?

MICHIYLA: I find it endearing.

(Julie-Ann looks at Michiyla with a puzzled and confused look.)

JULIE-ANN: Seriously?

MICHIYLA: Yes. To me, it shows that the person cares and wants to know.

(Julie-Ann resists the temptation to roll her eyes. Xaxbey senses a little irritation from Julie-Ann. He gently puts his hand on her shoulder.)

XAXBEY: That sure is true of Blake.

BLAKE: Yes. But I seem to ask all the questions at once instead of letting the person answer one before I ask another.

MICHIYLA: That's OK. I will probably have questions for you all too.

(Xaxbey hears static, and then a voice.)

HIS: Hey, Xaxbey. Michiyla was matched with Franklin, but it was discovered that he lied on his application.

XAXBEY: Ask all the questions you want. We have had some good conversations over here.

(Xaxbey looks over at Zarlow, nods, and points to the drink machine against the wall in sitting area four. Zarlow covertly nods back.)

ZARLOW: I'm gonna go get a drink. Anyone want to come with me?

(Clariese gets up.)

XAXBEY: I'm thirsty. I'll go.

(Xaxbey grabs Julie-Ann's arm.)

Julie-Ann, come with us.

(Julie-Ann feels Xaxbey pull her up almost out of the chair. She stands the rest of the way up. Ivirist looks at Anthony. He nods.)

IVIRIST: Anthony and I will come.

(The six of them leave, now it's just Blake, Michiyla, Grant, Everliegh, Braxton, and Yendizee. Braxton stands up.)

BRAXTON: I'm gonna go over to the old sitting area I used to hang out in. Anyone want to come?

(Braxton looks at Anthony. Yendizee jumps up.)

YENDIZEE: I'd like to see where you hung out.

BRAXTON: Cool. I'll introduce you to the folks over there.

(Braxton and Yendizee leave. Blake looks at Michiyla.)

BLAKE: Wow, did I scare everyone off again?

GRANT: Nah, they are just bored of sitting here like we all are.

BLAKE: I'm not bored.

GRANT: That's because you always have so many questions.

(Grant and Everliegh laugh. Everliegh looks over at Blake.)

EVERLIEGH: It's all good. Ask away, Blake.

BLAKE: Ha, ha. Most of my questions are prolly for Michiyla.

EVERLIEGH: That's OK. Hey, if she's OK with it, I'd like to hear the answers too.

(Everliegh looks over at Michiyla. Everliegh feels Grant grab her hand. Half expecting him to get up and drag her somewhere else, she is surprised when he sits back and tenderly rubs her fingers with his.)

MICHIYLA: That's fine with me. Pretty sure I have some questions too.

BLAKE: I'm glad my questions didn't put you off. Julie-Ann is right, I tend to go overboard with my inquisitiveness.

MICHIYLA: I'm glad you all invited me to sit here with you. Once I couldn't find Franklin, I wasn't sure what I was gonna do.

EVERLIEGH: Well, you're still here, so there's a reason.

(Everliegh looks over at Blake and winks. Blake smiles. Everliegh smiles at Grant.)

MICHIYLA: So, Everliegh, are you and Grant trying to match?

EVERLIEGH: Ha! Not when I first met him. Grant is a very self-absorbed person. Sometimes to the point of being a jerk.

GRANT: Hey!

(Everliegh elbows Grant in the side.)

EVERLIEGH: You know it's true!

(Grant shrugs. Then he nods.)

GRANT: It is. It's true.

MICHIYLA: But there's a possibility now?

(Everliegh looks at Grant. He smiles at her. Everliegh looks back over at Michiyla.)

EVERLIEGH: I suppose.

(Everliegh turns her head towards Grant and points at him.)

As long as he minds his manners!

(They all laugh.)

GRANT: Hey! I wasn't so sure of you either. When we first met, I thought you were a self-reliant, driven lady. We clashed a little, I think.

EVERLIEGH: You're not wrong. I am still those things, too. So, you better beware!

(Blake smiles as he takes in the conversation. He thinks back to the first time they all sat around and talked. His daydream is interrupted by Grant.)

GRANT: What about you Michiyla, are you in a hurry to find someone?

MICHIYLA: I don't know. Is Blake taken?

(They all giggle. Everliegh starts talking before Blake can.)

EVERLIEGH: I used to think he was gonna match with Yendizee. But we can see how that turned out.

(Everliegh points over to the drink machine where Yendizee and Braxton are talking to each other.)

GRANT: So, to answer your question, no, Blake is not taken.

MICHIYLA: That's good.

(Michiyla smiles at Blake. He smiles back.)

GRANT: Hey, Everliegh. Let's go get a snack. Maybe these two can catch up on life. And other things.

(Grant winks at Blake. Blake looks at Grant and mouths, 'thank you.')

EVERLIEGH: Good idea.

(Everliegh looks at Michiyla.)

Do you want anything?

MICHIYLA: No. I think I'm OK for now. Thank you.

EVERLIEGH: OK. If you need rescuing from all of Blake's questions, I'll be right over there.

(Everliegh points to the table twenty feet away with all of the snacks on it. They all laugh together, then Grant and Everliegh start to leave.)

MICHIYLA: Thanks. But I think I should be able to handle the many questions I sense are coming.

(Before Everliegh walks off, she goes over to Michiyla, leans down, and whispers in Michiyla's ear.)

EVERLIEGH: He's a good guy. Be gentle with him and he will give you the world.

(Michiyla nods and whispers.)

MICHIYLA: Got it, thanks.

(Blake watches as Everliegh and Grant leave. He feels himself getting nervous being somewhat alone with the new girl. He decides to make the first move.)

BLAKE: Hey, do you mind if I sit a little closer to you?

(Michiyla scooches over next to Blake. She turns to look at his face.)

MICHIYLA: I don't mind.

(Blake can feel the whole left side of his body touching Michiyla. He hesitates and decides not to touch her hand. Awkwardly, Blake starts asking Michiyla some questions.)

BLAKE: So, why did you choose this group over some of the others?

MICHIYLA: Mainly because a while back I saw that other lady, I think her name is Julie-Ann, walking around and talking to other people. She seems nice by the way.

BLAKE: You saw Julie-Ann here? That's why you stopped?

MICHIYLA: Yep. I recognized her. She's the only one in all the other sitting areas that I recognized.

BLAKE: Seriously? I would not have thought that.

MICHIYLA: Why?

BLAKE: Sorry, I didn't mean to…

MICHIYLA: Oh, no, it's no problem. I was just wondering why you thought that.

BLAKE: Oh. I…

(Michiyla interrupts Blake.)

MICHIYLA: Sorry, I didn't mean to put you on the spot.

(Blake leans a little closer to her.)

BLAKE: I'm usually the one asking the questions. I guess I'm not too good at answering them. Ironic isn't it?

(Michiyla giggles.)

MICHIYLA: It's kinda funny actually.

BLAKE: Right!

(Blake sits back a little.)

You're too cute to not have guys hitting on you all the time.

MICHIYLA: What?

(Michiyla turns to look at Blake again.)

BLAKE: I just meant... I umm... Ugh...

MICHIYLA: It's OK. I'm flattered. And kinda glad you think so.

BLAKE: Really? I was scared you were gonna hit me, or something.

MICHIYLA: You're funny. No. I won't hit you. I might slap you silly...

BLAKE: Ha! I might deserve that!

(They both laugh. Michiyla and Blake continue talking together for the rest of the day.)

END SCENE TWO

ACT 2

SCENE 3: CROSSROADS

(Julie-Ann is sitting beside Xaxbey in the love seat. Clariese and Zarlow sit at their normal table eating snacks and talking. Grant and Michiyla sit across from Julie-Ann and Xaxbey.)

JULIE-ANN: You two look like you have really hit it off.

BLAKE: Ya, all thanks to you.

(Blake leans back and puts his arm around Michiyla. She leans into him.)

JULIE-ANN: Really? Why?

BLAKE: Michiyla recognized you from the time you walked around the other sitting areas and talked to people. And because she recognized you, she stopped here with us.

JULIE-ANN: Awwww. That's so cool.

(Julie-Ann feels a little sick knowing she might be the one that helped them two get together. Julie-Ann feels her heart rate increase from the frustration and disappointment that suddenly overtakes her. Julie-Ann hears HRS start talking in her ear.)

KORISTINE: Julie-Ann, calm down.

(Julie-Ann shifts her weight wishing she could get away and talk to Koristine.)

Listen to me. Don't worry about what happens with Blake and Michiyla. We need to talk about you.

(Julie-Ann looks at Xaxbey and smiles trying to act cool while taking in everything Koristine is saying.)

You are getting close to having to make a choice. Are you wanting to move on to the next floor? Or do you want to go back to Floor One and start on the participants that will begin the process in a week? I know you can't answer me right now. But you need to make a choice soon.

(Julie-Ann's concentration is broken by Xaxbey's voice. Xaxbey elbows her in the ribs.)

XAXBEY: Hey! Julie-Ann! Are you listening?

JULIE-ANN: Huh? What?

XAXBEY: Are you OK? You were lost in space there for a second.

JULIE-ANN: Oh, ya. I'm fine.

(Julie-Ann smiles at him.)

What's going on?

XAXBEY: Blake was just giving you props over here. You normally enjoy being told you are right.

JULIE-ANN: Dang it! I'm sad I missed it! Say it all again!

(Julie-Ann nudges Xaxbey with her shoulder.)

XAXBEY: Too late now. You missed it.

(They all laugh a little. Xaxbey hears HIS in his ear.)

HIS: Dude, you are into her!

(Xaxbey smiles a little bigger.)

Anyway. Do you plan to go to the next floor or are you gonna call it quits at this location? This is your last rotation here, remember?

(The happy moment goes away in a hurry. Xaxbey's face turns serious.)

BLAKE: Are you OK, Xaxbey?

XAXBEY: Yes. I just got a little dizzy there for a sec.

JULIE-ANN: You need me to get you something?

XAXBEY: No. I might go lay down for a while though.

JULIE-ANN: You sure you're, OK?

XAXBEY: Yes. I'm fine. I'll be back in an hour or so.

(Xaxbey gets up and leaves. As soon as he is headed down the hallway to his room, he touches his ear.)

HIS, you there?

HIS: Yep.

(Xaxbey leans against the wall.)

XAXBEY: Are we already at that time?

HIS: Yes.

XAXBEY: If I choose to go back, and Julie-Ann goes back to Floor One, maybe I could go with her.

HIS: Xaxbey, you know that can't happen. She does not know about the "Maker" program.

XAXBEY: I could tell her.

HIS: No. You can't.

(Xaxbey crosses his arms.)

XAXBEY: Why not?

HIS: Do we need to go into this? You know you can't tell anyone. You'll get kicked out and you'll put her life in danger.

(Xaxbey walks down to his room. He opens the door and walks in. He imagines Julie-Ann waiting for him in a house of their own.)

XAXBEY: I have a feeling Julie-Ann could handle it. She wouldn't tell anyone.

HIS: No, Xaxbey.

XAXBEY: C'mon, man. I really like her.

HIS: I know. We can tell.

XAXBEY: Then, doesn't she deserve the chance to be trusted?

HIS: So, you are going to the next floor with her? Is that your choice?

XAXBEY: Can I tell her everything?

HIS: No.

XAXBEY: You aren't making this any easier.

(Xaxbey lays down on his bed.)

HIS: You know this is your job. You get paid to help participants. You don't get paid to fall in love.

XAXBEY: What happened when past Makers fell in love?

HIS: Xaxbey, you signed the NDA. You know what happens.

XAXBEY: So, I have to choose. Go to Floor Four, with Julie-Ann, or go to another 4S campus and start all over.

HIS: Yes. And if you stay here with and it doesn't work out, you will be sent back to Floor One to start over as a participant at a new location.

XAXBEY: You don't make this easy, do you?

HIS: You're the one that took this job.

XAXBEY: I never thought I'd be the one in love.

HIS: So, you admit it. You're in love with her!

XAXBEY: No! I mean. Well, yes, I guess so. Ugh. I'm 23 years old and I feel like I'm 13.

HIS: Butterflies, huh?

XAXBEY: Ya.

HIS: Well, you have a few days to think about it.

XAXBEY: OK. I will let you know when I figure it out.

(Xaxbey rolls over on his bed. He closes his eyes and dreams of Julie-Ann there cuddling with him. Meanwhile, Julie-Ann left Blake and Michiyla shortly after Xaxbey left. Julie-Ann made her way back to her room and is lying down

on her bed. With the pillow tucked comfortably under her head, she touches the back of her ear.)

JULIE-ANN: HRS, are you there?

KORISTINE: Yep. Right here with ya.

JULIE-ANN: I'm still pondering what I want to do.

(Koristine points to one of the techs below her. She covers the mic on her headset with her hand so Julie-Ann can't hear her.)

KORISTINE: You. Tech. Put Julie-Ann's vitals on the center tile.

TECH: Coming up in three… two… one…

(Julie-Ann's heat signature and heart rate appear on the center tile in the room. Stewart-Lee stares in awe once again.)

STEWART-LEE: That is so cool. Every time I see that I can't believe my eyes.

(Koristine glares at him like she has many times in the past.)

KORISTINE: Stewart-Lee, stop! You need to hush!

(Stewart-Lee bites his lip and turns around so he is not facing the tile. Koristine takes her hand off of her headset's mic.)

> Julie-Ann. I need you to think.

JULIE-ANN: About what? I'm getting tired.

KORISTINE: Do you want to go back to Floor One now?

JULIE-ANN: Ugh! I don't know!

(Julie-Ann pounds her fists into her bed. Koristine watches Julie-Ann's heartrate go up on the tile.)

KORISTINE: Do you want to stay here with Xaxbey for one more floor?

(Koristine waits for Julie-Ann to respond. Julie-Ann ponders the thought of staying with Xaxbey and seeing what happens. Koristine watches as Julie-Ann's heartbeat slows.)

> Julie-Ann?

JULIE-ANN: Huh? Oh. Ya.

KORISTINE: Ya, what?

JULIE-ANN: Umm. I'm not sure. Is there a chance I could get some more people to quit and get more credits?

KORISTINE: Yes. But remember, Floor Four is it. Then you go back to Floor One in the other building.

JULIE-ANN: I like this building better. The food tastes better here.

KORISTINE: That's it? Is that the only reason you want to stay?

(Koristine watches the tile as Julie-Ann's vitals race all over the place.)

What about...

(Julie-Ann waits for Koristine to finish her thought. But all she hears is silence. Finally, Koristine continues.)

Xaxbey.

(Julie-Ann smiles. Koristine watches as Julie-Ann's heat signature ticks up a bit on the tile.)

Hello?

(Julie-Ann snaps back to reality and answers Koristine.)

JULIE-ANN: What about him?

KORISTINE: Don't try to pull one over on me, Julie-Ann. You like him.

JULIE-ANN: First off, no.

(Koristine shakes her head and laughs.)

Secondly, I can't like anyone. I can't go to the Fifth Floor, right?

KORISTINE: Well, actually...

(Julie-Ann keeps going ignoring Koristine.)

JULIE-ANN: Third, even if I fell in love with a guy, I can't have a family in my job. And, well, I like my job. And then…

(Koristine cuts Julie-Ann off in a calm, soft voice.)

KORISTINE: Julie-Ann.

(Julie-Ann keeps rambling so Koristine yells into the mic.)

Julie-Ann!

JULIE-ANN: What! You don't have to yell at me!

KORISTINE: Shut up! Now, listen to me for a second.

JULIE-ANN: What?

KORISTINE: You might be able to go to Floor Five.

(Julie-Ann sits up a little on her bed.)

JULIE-ANN: Really?

KORISTINE: Yes.

(Julie-Ann pauses waiting for Koristine to explain how Floor Five might be a possibility. The momentary silence makes Julie-Ann nervous.)

JULIE-ANN: The silence makes me nervous. I feel like there is a…what do you call it?

KORISTINE: There is a stipulation.

JULIE-ANN: I knew it!

KORISTINE: And you might not like it, either.

JULIE-ANN: I figured that.

(Julie-Ann waits for Koristine to tell her.)

Well! C'mon. Tell me!

KORISTINE: Well. You will have to give up your job as a Destroyer.

(Julie-Ann sits all the way up on her bed.)

JULIE-ANN: Why?

KORISTINE: Remember your NDA you signed?

(Koristine starts quoting the NDA.)

"If anyone finds out…"

(Julie-Ann finishes the statement verbatim out of the NDA she memorized.)

JULIE-ANN: "…who the Destroyer is, or if the Destroyer tells anyone, both parties may be terminated. At the very least both individuals will be dismissed from the program."

(Julie-Ann takes a breath.)

I know. I know. Isn't there a way…

KORISTINE: Yes. That's the stipulation I was talking about. You have to give up your job as a Destroyer.

STEWART-LEE: I can take your place, Julie-Ann. I'm learning fast!

(Koristine glares at Stewart-Lee again. Julie-Ann starts yelling.)

JULIE-ANN: What is he still doing there? Get him out of this conversation!

(Stewart-Lee, realizing he is about to be in trouble with both Koristine and Julie-Ann, steps down off the platform and stands next to a tech. Koristine continues her conversation with Julie-Ann.)

KORISTINE: I'll take care of him.

JULIE-ANN: I am not giving up my job!

KORISTINE: Then you go to Floor One in the other building soon.

JULIE-ANN: OK. Fine.

(Julie-Ann plops back down on her bed. Not sure how she is feeling, she rolls over and looks up at the ceiling. She admits to herself she is in unchartered territory. Koristine speaks in a soothing manner once again.)

KORISTINE: Julie-Ann. Think about this long and hard. Do me a favor.

(Koristine stares at the tile with Julie-Ann's heat signature still showing.)

JULIE-ANN: OK.

KORISTINE: Think about Xaxbey.

(Julie-Ann smiles as she thinks of Xaxbey.)

Julie-Ann.

JULIE-ANN: Yes.

KORISTINE: Your heat signatures and heart rate just changed.

(Julie-Ann jumps off her bed,)

JULIE-ANN: Are you watching me? You better not be watching me!

KORISTINE: You know we can't see you. But the nanobots are still relaying vitals and your heat signatures.

(Julie-Ann walks over to the door and stands against it.)

We can still see your signatures. Even when you stand by the door.

(Julie-Ann huffs.)

JULIE-ANN: Fine!

(Julie-Ann goes back to her bed.)

KORISTINE: You like Xaxbey. Don't deny it. We can tell.

JULIE-ANN: Can just you and I talk?

(Koristine motions for the tech to cut off the monitor for the conversation. The tech gives a thumbs up to Koristine.)

OK. We are clear.

JULIE-ANN: What if I want both?

KORISTINE: How old are you, Julie-Ann?

JULIE-ANN: What's that got...

(Koristine interrupts her knowing exactly what she was going to say.)

KORISTINE: Just answer the question.

JULIE-ANN: 26.

KORISTINE: And how long have you been a Destroyer?

JULIE-ANN: You know my file better than I do.

KORISTINE: Answer please.

JULIE-ANN: Two and a half years.

KORISTINE: Now, here's the tricky part. Be completely honest with me. It's just you and me. No one is listening right now. This part of the conversation is not being monitored or recorded.

JULIE-ANN: OK.

KORISTINE: Do you like Xaxbey?

(Julie-Ann takes a deep breath, holds it, and slowly exhales.)

That tells you everything you need to know.

JULIE-ANN: How?

KORISTINE: How many times in the past have you ever thought about going past Floor Three or even Floor Four?

JULIE-ANN: None. I want to get back in there and do my job.

KORISTINE: Are you hearing yourself? This has never happened to you before. Do you think there might be something between the two of you?

(Julie-Ann takes a few moments to really ponder what Koristine said.)

JULIE-ANN: I suppose. Maybe.

KORISTINE: Julie-Ann. I think you are at a crossroads. There is nothing I can say or do to help you out. You have to consider this might be the time for you to take a chance and go through The Whole Seven Floors.

JULIE-ANN: I...

KORISTINE: I know. It's not easy. It's a tough choice.

(Julie-Ann puts her face in her hands.)

JULIE-ANN: Can I ask you a question?

KORISTINE: Sure.

JULIE-ANN: Have you gone through The Whole Seven Floors?

KORISTINE: Yes. It's a choice I had to make. It's hard. There are many advantages and disadvantages.

JULIE-ANN: So, I really have to make that same choice, huh.

KORISTINE: Yes, you do.

JULIE-ANN: And I can't tell him what I've been doing this whole time? I feel like if I don't, I'll be lying to him, in a sense.

KORISTINE: Can I start monitoring and recording this conversation again?

JULIE-ANN: Will it help?

KORISTINE: It might.

JULIE-ANN: OK, please start recording again.

(Koristine motions for the tech to put Julie-Ann's heat signature back up on the tile and to resume recording. The tech gives Koristine a thumbs up.)

KORISTINE: Ask your question again, please.

JULIE-ANN: Can I tell Xaxbey what I've been doing for the last two plus years?

KORISTINE: We are going to look into his background and decide if we feel he could keep the program a secret.

JULIE-ANN: Didn't I ask for that earlier?

(Koristine looks down at the tech off to her right. The tech nods back but shrugs her shoulders.)

KORISTINE: Yes, you did. We are still checking. We will put a rush on it, so you have time to decide what you want to do.

(Koristine motions for the tech to put a rush on it. The tech nods back and starts typing on her device.)

JULIE-ANN: OK, thanks. I guess I have some thinking to do.

KORISTINE: Yes, you do. Hey, Julie-Ann.

JULIE-ANN: Uh, huh.

KORISTINE: Good luck.

(Julie-Ann hears static and then it fades. She lays down on her bed unsure of what to do. For the first time ever, she is actually thinking of spending the rest of her life with one person. Julie-Ann shivers as goosebumps run up her arms. Then she feels something she has hardly ever felt before. There is a tingling and funny, yet surprisingly satisfying feeling in the depths of her stomach. Julie-Ann lays on her bed and stares at the ceiling.)

END ACT TWO

ACT 3

SCENE 1: ZARLOW MEETS HQ

(Enter Zarlow)

(Zarlow is in his room learning his new job. He is deep in the 4S mainframe looking around trying to determine the basic vulnerabilities of the system's programming. Zarlow is singing and humming to himself as he peruses around some of the less complicated coding. He stops when he sees the name, 'Xaxbey.')

ZARLOW: Xaxbey. Hum. Let's see who you are.

(As Zarlow digs into Xaxbey's file, he is surprisingly underwhelmed. Very little information is available. And what Zarlow does find is vague. Zarlow inserts a linear search algorithm with target element of 'Xaxbey.' As that search program is running, Zarlow implements another topic search, this time a binary search code is sent into the program with the target elements 'Maker, Xaxbey.' Hoping this search returns any array element with 'Xaxbey' as the middle element, Zarlow waits.)

C'mon. Where are you, Xaxbey?

(After a few seconds, a message returns. 'no search index is found, element count -0, target returning to home.' Zarlow scratches his head. Zarlow starts typing on his device. He

quickly creates an Auxiliary Space, no Time Complexity, Nano-Code search program with desired algorithmic patterns to match Data Encryption Standards and follow those paths to decrypt all personal, financial, and employment security information. Zarlow sets the return parameters to be 'Xaxbey--all.' Zarlow sits back and watches the nano program run through the 4S information. After a few minutes of seeing the same code over and over, Zarlow gets up and goes to the door. He looks out of the little peephole wishing Clariese was standing right outside. His dream is interrupted by a loud 'ding' that came from his device.)

ZARLOW: Finally. I got something.

(Zarlow walks back to his computer. In an instant of fear and dread, Zarlow covers his mouth. The device cursor is blinking as a message comes through.)

From HIS – Who are you?

(Zarlow ponders for a second. Should he answer? Zarlow realizes this person, or persons, already know he is there. Zarlow reluctantly starts typing his reply.)

From Zarlow – Who is this?

From HIS – This is the Human Intelligence Supervisor. Who are you?

From Zarlow – I am an employee of 4S. I have access to all programs within the 4S system. Let me get my supervisor so she knows you are impeding my desired outcomes.

(Zarlow starts another chat to try and get Koristine to help him alleviate this perceived roadblock. The cursor starts blinking again.)

From HIS – Who is your supervisor?

From Zarlow – I cannot tell you that per my NDA.

From HIS – Let me know your name and I will send it up the chain and see what I can do.

(Zarlow is unsure what an HIS is, but figures it can't hurt, Koristine can cover anything this person might try to dig up.)

From Zarlow – My name is Zarlow. I am a programming and coding Nano-Bio-ethical hacker and penetration tester for the 4S company.

(The cursor stops blinking.)

ZARLOW: Ha! That got you! Now stay outta my way!

(The cursor blinks again.)

From HIS – Ya, ummm. We don't show anyone in that sort of position.

From Zarlow – I'm new. Just started a few days ago. You want me to get my supervisor on here for you?

From HIS – Hold on. We are getting a message from HQ.

(Zarlow waits for a few seconds. He gets a one-word response.)

Proceed.

(The cursor stops.)

ZARLOW: Good riddance! Now let's see what is so important about Xaxbey that someone interrupted my programming.

(Zarlow resumes watching his code sift through the mass amounts of information. Another 'ding' comes from his device. Zarlow looks at the cursor. It's from Clariese.)

From Clariese – Hi Zee.

From Zarlow – Hi, my Clar Star.

From Clariese – I love it when you say I'm yours.

(Clariese sends a heart. Zarlow smiles. He sends two heart emojis back.)

Aaawwwwww.

(Clariese sends three heart emojis. Zarlow sends four more hearts back. They both smile as if the other could see them smiling.)

What are you doing?

From Zarlow – Trying to get some info and see what

kind of encrypted, anti-hacking, invisible blocker software the company has.

From Clariese – I have no idea what you just said. But, OK.

From Zarlow – I was also trying to find info on Xaxbey, and then some person interrupted me.

From Clariese – Who?

From Zarlow – Someone I've never heard of before. An HIS. You ever heard of that before?

From Clariese – Nope. New one to me.

From Zarlow – Not in your Destroyer time?

From Clariese – Nope. Never heard of that one.

From Zarlow – So if I was looking into Xaxbey, and he is the Maker, do you think it is a Maker supervisor?

From Clariese – Now that's an interesting thought.

From Zarlow – I'm gonna dig deeper.

From Clariese – Go get'em babe!

From Zarlow – Thanks! You know what?

From Clariese – What?

From Zarlow – I love you!

From Clariese – Aaawww. I love you too. I'd kiss you but you are far away.

From Zarlow – Technically, I'm not that far away.

From Clariese – Well, to me, you are far away.

From Zarlow – Mwah!

From Clariese – Back at ya, Zee. Let me know what you come up with. I'm gonna go get a drink and hang out with Michiyla and Blake. I really like them two.

From Zarlow – I'll let you know if I get anything. Have fun with Blake and Michiyla. Want me to spy on them for you? LOL.

From Clariese – No! Let them be. Michiyla has had a hard enough time already. She deserves someone like Blake.

From Zarlow – Fine, ruin all my fun. I'll be out in an hour or so. See you soon, my Clar Star!

From Clariese – See you soon, Zee.

(Zarlow watches as the cursor stops. He visualizes in his head how it will be when they are through The Whole Seven Floors, and he gets to spend all night with her. Zarlow lays back on his bed and waits for his program to finish running.)

ZARLOW: C'mon. Hurry up.

(No sooner did Zarlow finish talking, and another 'ding' comes through his device. It's Koristine.)

From Koristine – Zarlow. How's it going?

From Zarlow – Fine. How'd you know I was in here?

From Koristine – Our techs can still track you.

From Zarlow – Duh.

(Zarlow slaps himself on the forehead. He ponders how he can make his coding invisible to the HRS techs.)

> *Actually. I might need your help.*

From Koristine – OK, Hit me.

From Zarlow – Have you ever heard of HIS?

From Koristine – What?

From Zarlow – Someone who identified as Human Intelligence Supervisor found my program.

From Koristine – No, I've never heard of that one. Let me see what I can find. Give me a few minutes.

From Zarlow – Thanks.

From Koristine – Sure thing. Everything else going OK?

From Zarlow – Yep.

From Koristine – Everything good with Clariese?

From Zarlow – Yep.

From Koristine – You talked to her?

From Zarlow – Sure did. She's on board.

From Koristine – OK, I'll message you as soon as I hear anything about this HIS person.

From Zarlow – Thanks!

(Zarlow lays back down. Knowing his search program might take a few hours, he closes his eyes and starts to drift off to sleep. Just as he is about to fall deep asleep, he hears the cursor 'ding' again.)

From Koristine – Hey, Zarlow.

From Zarlow – Yes.

From Koristine – Not sure what or who HIS is, but you will be getting a message from HQ. I was told to stand down until HQ talks to you.

From Zarlow – Uh, OK. Should I be nervous?

*From Koristine – I don't think so. Just tell them you are

working for me on preventing internal and external data loss.

From Zarlow – OK. Thanks.

(Immediately Zarlow sees another cursor start. It reads, 'From HQ.' Zarlow closes the message string from Koristine and clicks on the message from HQ.)

From HQ – Is this Zarlow?

From Zarlow – Yes. Who is this?

From HQ – This is the 4S program Headquarters in Dalsastun.

Zarlow – How do I know you are who you say you are?

From HQ – We got a message from both HIS and Koristine wondering why you were in the 4S system.

From Zarlow – Oh. Ya, I talked to both of them today.

From HQ – Koristine told us what she has planned for you.

From Zarlow – Uh, huh.

From HQ – We are the ones who approved it.

From Zarlow – Really?

From HQ – You have access to all systems. You don't

really think Koristine could do that, do you?

From Zarlow – I guess that makes sense.

(Zarlow thinks for a second.)

Then who is HIS?

From HQ – They are the Maker's program supervisor. Just the same as Koristine is the Destroyer's supervisor.

From Zarlow – Why are there… how does…

(Zarlow is unerupted by HQ.)

From HQ – I know you have so many questions. Let's start with this. Your job is to make sure no one can get into our top-secret information. You have full access to all IT systems and platforms. We are updating your NDA. You will need to resign the document again. You remember how to sign it, right?

From Zarlow – Yes.

From HQ – Go ahead and do that and we can chat some more.

(Zarlow sees the cursor stop. He turns the device over and places his palm in the same spot. He feels the same sensation as last time, but he doesn't flinch this time. After the NDA is signed, he turns the device over and watches as words scroll across the device's screen. At the bottom,

Zarlow clicks on the icon "CLICK HERE." His DNA signature is processed almost instantaneously. The cursor starts blinking again.)

> *We have your signature. You are good to go. Good luck in all your endeavors. Any questions?*

From Zarlow – Yes. Only a couple for now.

From HQ – OK, I will do my best to answer them.

From Zarlow – I noticed in the new NDA, I cannot mention what I find out about HIS to the Destroyer or the HRS. Why is that?

From HQ – These two programs are intended to be separate in every way, except that they both work with the same set of participants to enhance and strengthen matched relationships. But they do it independently.

From Zarlow – I mean, I kinda understand that. But it also seems like they are working against each other.

From HQ – Yes, it does seem that way, but our organizational and relational psychiatrists and psychologists have determined this actually works for the best in our program. You have to keep our goal in mind. Strong families having fully functional families to increase the human population is what we are after here.

From Zarlow – I guess so.

From HQ – Your job is to prevent anyone from getting into our program and making the process, to include all sections and systems, publicly available.

From Zarlow – I think I can do that.

From HQ – Good. I knew you were the right person for the job. And Zarlow.

From Zarlow – Yes.

From HQ – You are not to inform either HRS or HIS of the existence of the other. They do not know that the other program is active. And it needs to stay that way.

From Zarlow – Yes, I think I saw something to that effect in the new NDA as I skimmed it while it scrolled across my device.

From HQ – OK good. You can work with them. But do it separately.

From Zarlow – Yep. I got it.

From HQ – Good.

(Zarlow starts typing, then hits the back space. Then he starts typing again. He deletes it. Nervous about asking any more questions, he finally enters his question.)

From Zarlow – What about Clariese? Oh, she's my...

(HQ starts typing.)

From HQ – Yes, we know. You two are good. She has been cleared to know everything. She was a good Destroyer and chose to enter the program after her last group. You don't think it was an accident we sent her to your floor, do you?

From Zarlow – Wow. I guess I never really thought...

From HQ – We plan things out very carefully around here. We knew your background, your tendencies, and your inquisitiveness. We knew you two would match perfectly. That's why we reintroduced her in your building, at just that time, and in that space.

From Zarlow – What if she didn't like me?

From HQ – After watching her as a Destroyer, we knew what sort of guy she would be attracted to.

From Zarlow – But how did you know she would see me?

From HQ – Zarlow.

From Zarlow – Yes.

From HQ – You're letting self-doubt show again. You are just the guy she needed and was looking for.

Ask Doc and Cook if they think she was not gonna see you and stop at your table.

From Zarlow – They had a hand in this too?

From HQ – Zarlow, they are a lot smarter than you think.

From Zarlow – Them suckers! I'm gonna get them.

(Zarlow smiles.)

From HQ – And if they failed, we always have Xaxbey.

From Zarlow – Yes, Xaxbey. What did he say to keep me in the program after I kissed Clariese? Hey, come to think of it. You weren't gonna dismiss me from the program, were you?

From HQ – That's Xaxbey's story to tell. I have a feeling you will find out what Xaxbey did. We had every intention of moving you to the other building and have you start over. You broke a rule, we didn't see that coming based on your background.

From Zarlow – Seriously? Wow. And thank you, Xaxbey!

From HQ – You might owe him more than you know. I need to go. If you need anything, just click on the blank home screen and type "HQ" and I will message you.

From Zarlow – OK, I'm sure I will have more questions.

From HQ – I have told you about everything I can. Zarlow, keep our information safe. We are counting on you.

(The cursor stops. Zarlow lays back down and closes his eyes.)

END SCENE ONE

ACT 3

SCENE 2: XAXBEY'S SACRIFICE

(Enter Zarlow)

(Zarlow is back in his room again. After spending the last few days with Clariese and hanging out with Michiyla and Blake, Zarlow decides to look further into Xaxbey's actions the day he was supposed to be dismissed from the program.)

ZARLOW: OK, program, let's go find this info.

(Zarlow sends out his encrypted spoofer program. He also watches his other programs identify vulnerabilities in the current coding. Zarlow notices a class function not completely written in the Destroyer program. Zarlow messages Koristine.)

From Zarlow – Koristine, I found a short code that needs fixed in the Destroyer program.

From Koristine – Hi, Zarlow. Can you fix it?

From Zarlow – Yes, I wasn't sure if I should or if one of your techs should do it.

(Koristine hears a voice come over the headset. She holds her hand up to the headset and listens. She gets word from one of the techs to have Zarlow do it.)

From Koristine – Go ahead and make the fix. Thanks for letting me know.

From Zarlow – Cool. This is an easy one. Thanks!

From Koristine – Sure thing.

(The cursor stops. Zarlow goes back to watching his program searching for Xaxbey's information run. He starts daydreaming, half watching the program and half off out in space somewhere when he sees what he has been looking for.)

ZARLOW: There you are. I found you!

(Zarlow starts reading the long paragraph about Xaxbey.)

"…and then he offered up his monthly credits to allow him to go to the next floor. When that wasn't enough, he offered his opportunity to go to Floor Four."

(Zarlow pauses. He scratches his head right behind his ear.)

I wonder who he gave up a whole month's worth of credits for?

(Zarlow keeps reading from the device.)

"The final agreement was that if the participant did not make it to Floor Three, Xaxbey would forfeit his job and leave the program."

(Zarlow sits up and stares at the wall for a moment.)

Holy moly! Xaxbey must be one heck-uv-a guy! Who would he sacrifice all that for?

(Zarlow sees his cursor start blinking.)

From Clariese – Hi. Zee.

From Zarlow – Hi, my Clar Star.

From Clariese – What are you doing?

From Zarlow – I found some interesting information.

From Clariese – Oh, do tell.

From Zarlow – Evidently, Xaxbey sacrificed a lot for a participant to stay in the program at one time. Like a whole lot.

From Clariese – Seriously? Why?

From Zarlow – I'm not sure. I'm still looking.

From Clariese – Let me know what you find.

From Zarlow – OK, I will. I think there's more I need to tell you too. Can we meet after I find what I'm looking for?

From Clariese – Of course. You want to meet in person?

From Zarlow – Ya, I think that would be best.

From Clariese – OK, you got one hour.

From Zarlow – Ha! You make me laugh. I'll do my best. See you in an hour. I love you.

From Clariese – I love you too, Zee.

(Zarlow watches the cursor until it stops blinking and goes away. He turns his attention back to the program searching Xaxbey's information.)

ZARLOW: C'mon, show me what I'm looking for.

(Zarlow watches as line after line of boring redundant code scrolls over his device. Then, in the middle of a code, something catches his eye.)

What is this?

(Zarlow follows the path of a code placed within another code to try and hide its existence. Zarlow opens it up. Excitement comes over every inch of his body.)

Finally! I found something.

(Zarlow starts reading out loud again.)

"Entry 151 of Xaxbey, Maker for participant list 1,356. 'I offered as much as I could for Zarlow today. He kissed a lady and the 4S program's nanobots caught him. Before the guards could take him away, I talked with HIS to try and prevent

> Zarlow from being dismissed. I have a good feeling about this kid. I think he found his perfect match. I had to do everything I could. I finally reached an agreement with HIS, or maybe even someone higher, I'm not sure, just to keep him in the program.

(Zarlow shakes his head. He mutters as he rereads the last paragraph.)

> No way. Why would he do that?

(Zarlow switches screens on his device and messages Clariese.)

From Zarlow – Clariese, are you still there?

(Zarlow waits for a few seconds. When he doesn't get a response, he closes the message screen. He opens the codes he has running and stops them. After he is sure they have returned and no trace of his programs can be found, Zarlow races out of his room, down the hall, and into the sitting area where Clariese normally is.)

ZARLOW: Where is she?

(Zarlow looks around to see if he can spot Clariese. She is nowhere to be seen. Zarlow sits at the table with the food, grabs a plate, and eats a few pieces of fruit. He feels a hand on his shoulder.)

CLARIESE: Hi, Zee.

(Zarlow turns and looks at her.)

ZARLOW: Hello, my Clar Star.

(Zarlow blows her a kiss. She grabs the air as if to grab his kiss and hold on to it.)

CLARIESE: How are you?

ZARLOW: I am a bit perplexed.

CLARIESE: How so?

ZARLOW: Let's go sit in the corner and talk.

(Clariese and Zarlow go over to the corner where they can talk without the nanobots relaying their visual information into the 4S mainframe.)

CLARIESE: What's this all about?

ZARLOW: I found out a lot about Xaxbey. I'm not even sure where to start.

CLARIESE: How about…

(Zarlow keeps talking without realizing Clariese was talking too.)

ZARLOW: And I even learned some things about you, And about me. And about us!

CLARIESE: Wait, what?

ZARLOW: See, I told you. Where do I start?

CLARIESE: Probably from the beginning. That way the pieces all fall into place, right?

(Zarlow scooches closer to Clariese, and puts his hand on her thigh, right above her knee. Clariese watches as his hand rubs her thigh and then his fingers start circling around her knee. She leans back against the wall enjoying the sensation of his hand on her leg.)

ZARLOW: Where was I? I got lost there for a second.

CLARIESE: You are gonna tell me all about Xaxbey.

XARLOW: Oh yes. OK.

(Zarlow continues circling Clariese's knee with his thumb and forefinger.)

CLARIESE: Zee!

ZARLOW: Ok, fine!

(Zarlow puts the palm of his hand on Clariese's knee and starts to tell her what he learned.)

So, what I learned is that your being sent to Floor One with me was no accident. Somehow, the program had us matched before we even met.

CLARIESE: How? I was a Destroyer.

ZARLOW: I guess when you decided to get out of the Destroyer program, the algorithm automatically ran your DNA. Come to find out, I just happen to match with you.

CLARIESE: Well, thank goodness!

ZARLOW: Right!

(Zarlow squeezes Clariese's knee. She smiles and puts her head on his arm.)

CLARIESE: Keep going.

ZARLOW: OK, after they, whoever "they" are, found this out, they planned out how you and I would meet. I was told that they even looked into my background and knew I would like you.

CLARIESE: How do you know that?

ZARLOW: Know what?

CLARIESE: That someone looked into your background.

ZARLOW: Oh ya. So, I was contacted by the 4S program's Headquarters.

(Clariese sits up straight and looks at Zarlow.)

CLARIESE: Who is that?

ZARLOW: The head boss over the HRS.

CLARIESE: There's a boss over HRS?

(Clariese tilts her head, looks straight ahead, and then returns her focus back to Zarlow.)

ZARLOW: Yep. And HQ talked with me.

CLARIESE: What did they say?

ZARLOW: That's what I am telling you. I'm telling you what they said.

CLARIESE: Oh, OK. Well, keep going!

ZARLOW: So, when they found out that we were a DNA match, they arranged it so you would come over to the sitting area I was at first.

CLARIESE: We were set up!

ZARLOW: I mean, I guess so. Sort of.

CLARIESE: Zee! They set it up, so we didn't even have a choice!

ZARLOW: Well, even if I had a choice, I'd still choose you. From the moment I saw you, I knew I wanted to be with you.

CLARIESE: You would hardly even look at me!

ZARLOW: I know. But that doesn't mean I didn't want to be with you.

(Zarlow starts circling Clariese's knee with his fingers again. Clariese leans against Zarlow.)

CLARIESE: It's weird, because as soon as I saw you, I knew the same thing.

ZARLOW: Like all the DNA mapping and checking they did was spot on.

CLARIESE: Yes. But still. We were set up!

(Clariese puts her hand on Zarlow's.)

Anyway. Tell me more.

ZARLOW: Doc and Cook also played a part in getting us together.

CLARIESE: You know, now that you say that; I remember Doc escorting me to the door and showed me the area you were in.

ZARLOW: That makes sense. HQ told me if I had any questions about how our meeting was arranged to ask Cook and Doc.

CLARIESE: I can't believe they did that!

ZARLOW: Right! But I'm glad they did.

(Zarlow looks at Clariese and peers into her eyes. He dreams of the day when he can kiss her in public. Or anywhere for that matter.)

CLARIESE: That's kinda creepy though. And what would happen if we didn't get along?

ZARLOW: They mentioned they knew the type of guy you would look for, and if all else failed, they had Xaxbey to ensure we got together.

CLARIESE: So, we didn't really have a choice? It's a good thing I like you, Zee!

(They look at each other and laugh. Zarlow yields to the temptation and gives her a peck on the lips. Then he continues.)

ZARLOW: What's even crazier is what Xaxbey had to do to keep me in the program.

CLARIESE: Huh?

ZARLOW: Do you remember when I kissed you on the cheek and they took me away?

CLARIESE: How could I forget that? And yet, it almost seems like a lifetime ago.

ZARLOW: Well, when Xaxbey went and talked to the Guards, evidently, they also talked with HQ. Clariese, check this out. Xaxbey had to give up a lot to keep me here.

CLARIESE: Like what?

ZARLOW: He gave up a month's worth of credits. And check this out too, if we didn't make to Floor Three, he offered to leave the program!

CLARIESE: What?

ZARLOW: I'm serious! If we wouldn't have made it here, Xaxbey would be gone.

CLARIESE: Zee, we need to say thanks! We owe him big time!

ZARLOW: Right! I was thinking the same thing.

CLARIESE: What can we do for him?

ZARLOW: I'm working on that. He did a lot for me. I think I have a way to pay him back.

CLARIESE: Really. How?

ZARLOW: I'm still planning it, but he and Julie-Ann are getting close. I'm not sure if they will make it to Floor Four. Maybe there is a way to get them both there.

CLARIESE: That would be nice. But how? She is a Destroyer. And he is Maker. Are you gonna tell them about each other?

ZARLOW: I thought about that. But I don't think I can. HQ told me they act independently and can't know about each other.

CLARIESE: Oh, ya, that's tough.

ZARLOW: Unless…

(Clariese looks at Zarlow and finishes his sentence.)

CLARIESE: Unless they are cleared to know about each other. Kinda like we are cleared to know all of this.

ZARLOW: Exactly! Except…

(Clariese finished his thought again.)

CLARIESE: …if that happens, and one doesn't agree, they are both out of the program, or worse.

ZARLOW: Yes, that might be true. What do I do? How can we help them without jeopardizing their careers, or even their lives?

CLARIESE: Let's think about it.

(Clariese taps Zarlow on the shoulder and points straight ahead.)

There's Xaxbey. He's coming this way.

(Zarlow hollers over to Xaxbey.)

ZARLOW: Hey! Xaxbey! Come over here!

(Xaxbey looks over and sees Zarlow and Clariese sitting in the corner. He walks over to them.)

Have a seat, my friend.

XAXBEY: OK.

(Xaxbey sits down and looks at Clariese and Zarlow.)

        What's up?

ZARLOW: I'm not sure how to say this.

(Sensing Zarlow hesitate a little, Clariese jumps right in.)

CLARIESE: Thank you for everything you did to keep Zarlow in the program when he was taken out by the guards.

XAXBEY: Oh, no big deal.

CLARIESE: Actually, we know it was a big deal. And we wanted to say thanks.

ZARLOW: Ya, we appreciate all you did to keep me here. We are grateful for the confidence you have in Clariese and I.

XAXBEY: Hey, you know, I'm just doing my job.

CLARIESE: You gave up way more than…

(Zarlow gently nudges Clariese. She stops.)

ZARLOW: We appreciate all you did. We would love to be able to repay you someday. If you ever need anything, please let us know.

XAXBEY: There is no need. I'm just happy for the two of you.

CLARIESE: Are you and Julie-Ann still getting along? You kinda look cute together.

(Clariese reaches across Zarlow and pushes Xaxbey with her finger.)

XAXBEY: Oh, I don't know. I like her, a little. But you know, I don't know how far it can go.

ZARLOW: Well, if we can help you two at all, just ask. We owe you.

XAXBEY: Thanks. I'm sure it will all work out OK. I'm just happy for you two and how far you have come.

(Xaxbey gets up and looks at Zarlow and Clariese. He winks and walks off. Clariese looks at Zarlow.)

CLARIESE: We have to do something for him.

END SCENE TWO

ACT 3

SCENE 3: ZARLOW'S CHOICE

(Enter Zarlow)

(Zarlow is in his room waiting for Clariese to come online. He plays a few games and searches for more incomplete and faulty code. Zarlow thinks back to his conversation with HQ. It's been a few days, and the time to move to Floor Four is almost here.)

ZARLOW: I wonder how much of what that individual at HQ said was true. I think I might try to chat with him again.

(Zarlow hears a click. He looks down at his device and sees the cursor is active. He waits to see who it is.)

From Clariese – Hi, Zee. Have you thought about what we can do for Xaxbey?

From Zarlow – Hi, my Clar Star. I have been thinking about it a lot. I was about to message HQ and see what they thought.

From Clariese – Have you thought about looking around in Xaxbey's information some more first?

From Zarlow – I think I've been through most of it.

From Clariese – Did he keep any personal notes? Or recorded conversations with his boss?

From Zarlow – Ya know what, I'm not sure. I'll check that out. Thanks, Clar Star.

From Clariese – You're welcome. We make a great team!

From Zarlow – I agree! Hold on a second.

(Zarlow sets out a search program with "Xaxbey Notes" as the parameters.)

> *I just set out a search for any notes Xaxbey might have put in the system.*

From Clariese – How long will it take?

From Zarlow – I'm not sure.

(As soon as Zarlow hit send on his message, his search returned with zero matches.)

> *Or about that long. My search came back with nothing. Let me try another search.*

From Clariese – Hopefully this search will find something we can use.

From Zarlow – I'm looking for any conversations he had with HIS. Maybe I can pick something up from there.

From Clariese – Let's hope so.

(Zarlow lets the search run for a while. He sees the return results.)

From Zarlow – Well, there are certainly a lot of conversations here. I'm going to narrow my search down to conversations about Julie-Ann.

From Clariese – Why just her? Could there be others too?

From Zarlow – I suppose, but I figured I'd start there.

From Clariese – That would make it easier for us if there was some sort of talk about her in there.

From Zarlow – Give me a minute and then I'll let you know what comes back.

From Clariese – You know I'd wait forever for you.

(Zarlow feels his cheeks flush. He puts his hand on his face. His cheek feels hot and sweaty just like the first time he saw Clariese.)

From Zarlow – You are the best thing that ever happened to me.

From Clariese – Same. We kinda rock.

From Zarlow – Ya, we kinda do, don't we?

(Clariese sends a kissing emoji.)

From Clariese – Someday I am gonna kiss you for real.

From Zarlow – Mmmmmm. I can't wait. That is something I'm excited for.

(Clariese smiles. She visualizes being held in Zarlow's arms.)

From Clariese – What else are you excited for?

(Zarlow panics. He whispers out loud to himself.)

ZARLOW: What do I say? No one has ever talked to me like this before or asked me a question like this. C'mon Zee, think.

(Zarlow starts typing quickly so Clariese doesn't get any bad ideas.)

From Zarlow – You know what, with you, I'm excited for EVERYTHING!

From Clariese – Me too, Zee. Me too!

(Zarlow sees the search return with some parts of recorded conversations with HIS. Zarlow starts sending them to Clariese.)

From Zarlow – I found some. Check these out. This is from HIS to Xaxbey.
"Dude, you are into her."

From Clariese – That's it?

From Zarlow – So far. I'm still looking. At least we know the nanobots have picked up enough from his vitals to know that he likes Julie-Ann a little bit.

(Zarlow sits up on his bed. Trying to come up with a way to find out more, he moves so that his back is against the wall. He leans against the wall and closes his eyes.)

From Clariese – Hey, Zee. I have an idea.

(Clariese waits for Zarlow to start typing. The cursor doesn't appear.)

Zee.

(Clariese waits for a few seconds more.)

Hey! Zee!

(Zarlow opens his eyes and sees the messages from Clariese.)

From Zarlow – Hi. Yes?

From Clariese – Are you OK?

From Zarlow – Yes. I had my eyes closed. Sorry.

From Clariese – And what were you thinking about?

From Zarlow – You and me. Together. You know.

From Clariese – Don't lose that thought. We might need to talk about that some more later, I think.

(Clariese blushes sending that message.)

But for now, I have an idea.

From Zarlow – About my thoughts?

From Clariese – Well, yes. That too.

(Zarlow feels his face and ears get hot again.)

From Zarlow – Yay! We should definitely explore that topic.

From Clariese – Yes, but for now, stop! Focus!

From Zarlow – I feel like I was pretty focused.

(Clariese smiles. She feels the butterflies in her stomach again.)

From Clariese – I mean about my idea!

(Zarlow let's himself start to fantasize about Clariese. He shakes his head to try and bring himself back to reality.)

Zee!

From Zarlow – Yes. Ok. I'm here. What's your idea?

From Clariese – Can you search for conversations by Julie-Ann? Maybe she likes Xaxbey? Maybe the nanobots caught some signs showing she likes him too?

From Zarlow – You are so smart! Maybe you should be the coder and investigator.

(Clariese shakes her head.)

From Clariese – No thanks. That's your job.

(Clariese sends Zarlow a wink emoji. Zarlow types up some search terms and sends out a search code to find the conversations Julie-Ann had about Zarlow.)

From Zarlow – OK, I sent out the code. Let's see what we can find.

(Zarlow and Clariese talk about the future and other lighthearted topics. After 15-20 minutes, Zarlow receives the search results.)

I got the results.

From Clariese – And?

From Zarlow – Holy moly. There are more than a few times the HRS mentioned to Julie-Ann that her heat signature goes up when she's around Xaxbey.

From Clariese – That's a good thing, right?

From Zarlow – *For us maybe. But what does that mean for her job?*

From Clariese – *Oh ya. That's a good point. A Destroyer can't fall in love.*

From Zarlow – *When does the Destroyer go back to Floor One?*

From Clariese – *I think after Floor Four. If I remember correctly.*

(Clariese tries to remember back if she ever made it to Floor Five.)

From Zarlow – *Well, we know that Xaxbey and Julie-Ann like each other. Now we have to figure out how to tell them without ruining their jobs or their lives.*

(Just as Zarlow sent the message to Clariese, another cursor started blinking. It is HQ.)

From HQ – *Mr. Zarlow.*

From Zarlow – *HQ.*

From HQ – *We see you are looking into Xaxbey and Julie-Ann.*

From Zarlow – *Yes.*

From HQ – *Is there some code that needs fixed in those search terms?*

From Zarlow – Not that I've found.

From HQ – So what's the reason you are in those areas?

From Zarlow – Well. To be completely honest…

(HQ interrupts.)

From HQ – Yes. Please be honest.

From Zarlow – OK. Well, I found the amount of sacrifice Xaxbey made for me. I also found that he likes Julie-Ann. And further, Julie-Ann likes him too.

From HQ – So. Why are you looking there?

From Zarlow – I would like to repay Xaxbey for all he did for Clariese and I.

From HQ – Zarlow, you are the kindest guy at that compound. A big reason why we wanted to hire you. But be careful what you ask for, you might not like the answer, and you might just get it anyway.

From Zarlow – What does that mean?

From HQ – You know if the Destroyer is discovered, he or she is dismissed from the program, and possibly terminated.

From Zarlow – But what if they were deemed capable of

keeping the secret? Kinda like Clariese and I.

From HQ – That is a huge risk, Zarlow.

From Zarlow – Does it matter if I think they would handle it appropriately and professionally?

From HQ – No, Zarlow. We don't deal in good words and hopes.

From Zarlow – So what can I do to help them? They would make a great couple.

From HQ – Like I said, we don't deal in hopes and dreams.

From Zarlow – So, what is it you deal in? I have credits. I could cover the cost of hiring a new Destroyer if Julie-Ann doesn't make it.

From HQ – We have all the credits we need, Zarlow. What we need is good Destroyers and Makers.

From Zarlow – OK, so how can I help?

From HQ – Be careful, Zarlow. You won't like the cost of your request.

From Zarlow – I lived with my parents. I have more credits than I know what to do with. Name your price.

From HQ – You are willing to risk what we ask for Xaxbey?

From Zarlow – I think so.

From HQ – This will not only cost you. But Clariese too.

(Zarlow thinks for a second. This might change things. He doesn't want to risk anything to do with Clariese. He would never do that. But what if she wanted to be a part of this? Zarlow types back to HQ.)

From Zarlow – Can you invite her into this conversation? She and I have been on the same page almost all of the time. I think she would support helping Xaxbey.

From HQ – Per your request, Clariese is here.

(Zarlow sees Clariese's name pop up in the thread.)

From Zarlow – Hi, Clariese.

From Clariese – Ummm. Hi.

From Zarlow – HQ is on this thread. We are about to find out what it will take to help Xaxbey and Julie-Ann get together.

From Clariese – And you needed me for that?

From Zarlow – Yes. HQ says the price will not just cost me, but you too,

From Clariese – OK. I'm ready.

(Clariese feels herself getting nervous.)

From HQ – Clariese. Zarlow. It is admirable that you want to help Xaxbey and Julie-Ann match. Because one is a Maker and the other a Destroyer we cannot just tell them about each other. That could have great implications to the integrity of the 4S program. Since this will be such a big risk, we will require much from you.

From Zarlow – I think we are ready.

From HQ – As we said, we don't deal in credits. The cost for us to risk bringing Xaxbey and Julie-Ann into this relationship, is your future.

From Zarlow – That's it? How so? What is it you want from my future?

(Clariese covers her mouth scared of what HQ might be requesting.)

From HQ – If Julie-Ann and Xaxbey do not make it through The Whole Seven Floors, you will forfeit your job. You will also be placed in a remote location with no further communication with your family or friends. You will have no access to 4S or its information. Any attempt to regain access will cause forfeiture of life. Zarlow, you will have nothing. And you will have no way of gaining any resemblance of what you have now.

From Zarlow – Clariese, what do you think?

From Clariese – Can I help Zarlow in getting Xaxbey and Julie-Ann through the process?

(The cursor stops for a second. Then Clariese sees it start blinking again.)

From HQ – That is acceptable.

From Clariese – If it doesn't work, am I allowed to go to the remote location with Zarlow?

From Zarlow – What? No!

From Clariese – Zee, I only want to be with you. Here, or any other place, it doesn't matter. As long as I'm with you, that's all I care about.

From Zarlow – I could not ask that of you.

From Clariese – You did not ask. I offered.

(HQ interrupts Zarlow and Clariese's conversation.)

From HQ – Let me check to see if that would be acceptable.

From Zarlow – You are willing to sacrifice that much with me to get Xaxbey together with Julie-Ann?

From Clariese – Zee, I'm in it with you. Whatever you decide, I support one hundred percent.

From Zarlow – Are you sure? We could be banished to a baren island.

From Clariese – As long as we are together, I don't care.

From HQ – It has been decided that Clariese may help. If, however, it does not work, you both will be dismissed and sent away to a location of our choice.

From Zarlow – But we will be together, right?

From HQ – If that is what you both agree to. If you choose not to help Xaxbey and Julie-Ann, we will guarantee you and Clariese are married. Zarlow, you will have any job in the 4S coding department you want. Clariese, we will offer you any supporting job you want. All you have to do is tell us what job you want.

From Zarlow – So, we can have the jobs of our dreams and be married. Or we can risk it all to try and help Xaxbey?

From HQ – That is the agreement.

From Clariese – That's a big decision, Zee. We need to think about this.

From Zarlow – I agree, this is a huge decision. We can

> *have a safe and secure future together, or we can try and help Xaxbey. I know what I want to do. I have already made up my mind. I just want to know how you feel.*

From Clariese – I've never had a sure thing like this before. It is tempting to take the deal. Xaxbey and Julie-Ann are smart individuals.

From HQ – You can take as long as you need to decide.

(Clariese and Zarlow ignore HQ.)

From Clariese – Are we really willing to give up a guaranteed future?

From Zarlow – Clariese, I wouldn't be this far if it wasn't for Xaxbey. I need to take this chance.

From Clariese – I support you, Zee.

From HQ – So you have made your choice?

From Clariese – I think we have.

From HQ – Zarlow?

From Zarlow – Yes.

From HQ – You can review the agreement on your device.

From Zarlow – I got it. Should I send it to Clariese?

From HQ – Yes. She needs to read and sign it too.

(Zarlow sends the contract to Clariese. Together, Clariese and Zarlow review the agreement. They discuss the choice that is in front of them. Together they sign the NDA. With work to do, they set out to try and get Xaxbey and Julie-Ann to match together.)

END ACT THREE

Thank you so much for reading Floor Three. Would you please leave a review for me? I would love to know what you think about the book. Be sure to continue the saga and follow Zarlow and Clariese in "The 4S Project: Floor Four."

Made in the USA
Monee, IL
13 November 2024